jim armstrong
danny franzreb
jd hooge
ty lettau
lifaros
keith peters
paul prudence
jared tarbell
brandon williams

fresh flash

new design ideas with Flash MX

credits

authors
jim armstrong
danny franzreb
jd hooge
ty lettau
lifaros
keith peters
paul prudence
jared tarbell
brandon williams

technical reviewers
marco baraldi
leon cych
steve mccormick
mike sloan
jared tarbell

indexer
simon collins

managing editor
ben huczek

commissioning editor
jim hannah

editors
jon bounds
alan mccann
ben renow-clarke
victoria blackburn

designer
katy freer

author agent
chris matterface

project manager
jennifer harvey

proof readers
kristian besley
cathy succamore

mega shouts out to ben and kristian for being wonderkids!

fresh flash
new design ideas with Flash MX

First printed August 2002

ISBN 978-1-59059-190-1   ISBN 978-1-4302-5163-7 (eBook)
DOI 10.1007/978-1-4302-5163-7

contents

Jim Armstrong

Mr. Armstrong is a 3D animator specializing in Character Animation, Particle FX, and Digital Video. He is a four-time winner of a Creative Excellence Award at the International Web Page Awards, including 'Best Audio/Video', 'Best Personal Site' in 2000 and 'Best Personal Site' in 2001. He was a finalist in 'Best Use of Video' at the 1999 South by Southwest Interactive Festival and a finalist in the Video category at the NY 2002 Flash Film Festival.

Mr. Armstrong is a contributing writer to the 3D Cafe VIP Lounge and a moderator in the 3D Forum at Ultrashock.

Danny Franzreb

Danny is founder and art director of TAOBOT, an award-winning studio that specializes in interactive design and application development. Although studying economics and information technology, he has kept a vivid passion and drive for design. Being able to build what he designs and vice versa, exploration in both directions is what he enjoys most. Currently residing in Alsheim, Germany, Danny has become a frequent writer and speaker on the topic of Flash development, which gives him the possibility to meet inspiring people all over the world. In his spare time, he serves as a moderator for the Flashkit forums and explores new grounds with his personal website franzreb.com.

JD Hooge

After graduating from design school in 2000, I started the Fourm Design Studio with 3 close friends. After 2 years of focus and dedication to design and intraction, the co-founders of Fourm dispersed into different realms of the design field. Now I'm doing freelance work from my home-office, working on a few book projects (like this one), lots of side projects (gridplane.com, infourm.com, miniml.com) and cruising around in Craig's (miniml.com) '76 GMC Sprint.

Ty Lettau

Ty operates a site called soundofdesign.com which explores and experiments with the possibilities of interactive media. He also teaches design part-time at the Milwaukee Institute of Art and Design. Ty has been nominated for three Flash Film Festival Awards and has been featured in several web design magazines. Ty has recently created projects for VectorLounge (vectorlounge.com/04_amsterdam/jam/soundofdesign.html) and Born Magazine (bornmagazine.org/projects/core) as well as writing a chapter for friends of ED's Flash Math Creativity and contributing a photographic essay to the Backyard Project book

Lifaros

I'm an ActionScripter from Chile. There aren't many of us AS coders here, and there aren't many ActionScript jobs either, so I started searching for clients on the Internet instead, developing some applications, and participating on Flash forums. I have a lot of hobbies – sometimes I work as an electronics engineer on satellite communications and networking, sometimes I work as a painter and sculptor. As you can see, I love both art and math. Nowadays I work as a freelance ActionScripter for people from the USA and United Kingdom, and I also develop educational Flash math work for a company in Norway. Lifaros' own experimental flash gallery can be found at www.actionscript.cl

Keith Peters

I live in Lynn, Massachusetts with my wife Kazumi. I've been using flash off and on for nearly three years now, but far more heavily in the last year. My personal site, www.bit-101.com launched in August 2001, and I strive to keep up with the experiment-a-day schedule. It features fairly simple graphics, usually relying on math and scripting to build complex forms and movements.

Paul Prudence

The core of my time as an artist is spent making photons answer the call of simple mathematical equations and abstract forms recombine according to the movement of the mouse. Flash is a uniquely beautiful program that allows a perfect merge of both aesthetic concerns and math. It allows me to produce complex replicative forms with relative ease and system templates that can be tweaked often resulting in surprising new forms. In this sense structures and systems produced are often cultivated over period of succesive generations of code – splicing lines of code from here and there and grafting into new code sequences. I suppose about 10% of my experiments in Flash find their way onto my personal experimental space, transphormetic.com. When not lost in artistic adventure, I pay the rent and keep alive by working as a freelance creative developer/designer - examples of this kind of work can be found at slightspace.com. When working on client projects I am always looking for some artistic use of a commercial solution, the reverse is also true, some creative tinkering in flash can provide solutions for a lot of commercial projects.

Jared Tarbell

When I was 18, I decided to buy a computer instead of a car. That was back in 1991. I did this also in 1993, 1995, and again this year. To me, this is an absolutely brilliant thing to do - at least until cars can fly. Even before I owned a computer, in some form or another, I have been borrowing CPU time on other people's computers. I was initially motivated to use the computer through the text based adventure games my father would write while I was asleep. It became clear to me that a programmer truly could create something from nothing, and this idea intrigued me. I completed the ten year program at New Mexico State University and was rewarded a Bachelor of Science in Computer Science for my participation in their experiment. During this time I learned the value of abstracted programming and why I never want to program at a micro level.

Brandon Williams

Michael Brandon Williams is a freshman year Mathematics major at New York University. His mathematics focus has been real analysis, graph theory, combinatorics, and number theory. His computer science experience is based on programming design, object-oriented programming, and problem solving. In his spare time, he helps run the math forum at Were-Here (www.were-here.com) under the name of ahab, and works for Eyeland Studios (www.eyeland.com) as a games programmer.

The most exciting artwork in any medium is created by those pushing at its boundaries – but what happens when the goalposts are moved? What will the great Flash artists create with the new MX functionality?

With this book, we take a snapshot of exactly what designers are up to with their new toy. From the drawing API, to the fantastic sound and video support, these designers are dying to share their MX-citement and inspirations – and of course their code!

Since we're dealing with techniques and features new to Flash, each of the chapters in this book will teach new script and new techniques. Each new feature is explained, before the chapters dive off into a sea of iterations and design fantasy.

If you're looking to gain a sensitivity to MX, this is the place. All of the chapters have a wealth of script for you to investigate, changing values in some of these FLAs will radically alter the effects – cranking them up will really test the power of your CPU, and maybe your eyes and brain too!

The designers contributing to this book have created sites in previous versions of Flash that have astounded and stretched what people have thought possible with the tool. Now we present the chance to watch over their shoulders as they delve into the new super-powerful Flash MX!

You can download the source files from www.friendsofed.com/books/flash_mx_titles/fresh_flash/code.html

drawing api

keith peters

My whole life I've been into drawing. I have very early memories of family and friends telling me I should be an artist. In my younger days it was cartoon characters from MAD Magazine; in my teens it was realistic portraits of my favorite rock stars. I was never much into color, mostly using pencil or black ink. Although I never went into art as a career, I was always doodling an drawing, and in the mid-90s made a bit of money doing pen and ink illustration.

So it's not surprising that when I first got my hands on a computer in 1986 – a Commodore 128 – I was most awed by its ability to draw pictures. The Commodore's operating interface was itself a form of the BASIC programming language. I soon learned how to draw lines and turn them into basic shapes. I remember the two things that awed me the most on that computer: One was a map of the United States drawn in code. It was an array of coordinates and a FOR loop containing line drawing commands. The other one was a similar array that used the setPixel command to draw a bitmap of a human eye. This idea of using programming and numbers to draw cool pictures really stuck with me, and was the seed that later bloomed into the work I do on www.bit-101.com.

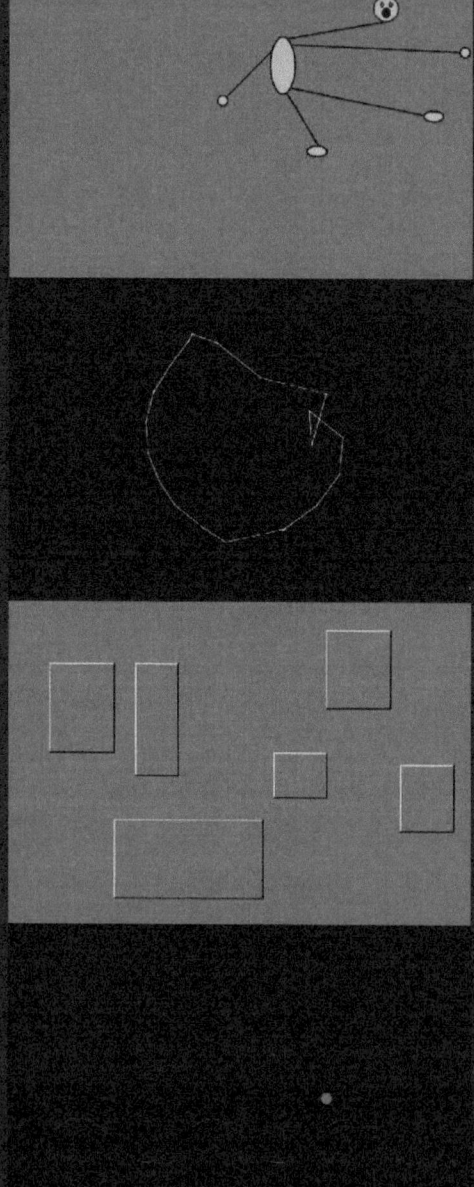

Over the years, I moved to a Commodore Amiga and eventually into the world of the PC. I made a few attempts at learning C and C++ and some other languages. During that time, I had two passions – computers and drawing. But for some reason, they never connected. They were two separate parts of my life. I played around with Paint Shop Pro and various 3D modeling programs, but the computer-art connection never clicked. Even when I first discovered Flash and started doing some web work with it, it was just another interesting application to learn and use and make money with.

Then one day I discovered ActionScript and my whole viewpoint shifted. I was transported back to the days of that Commodore 128 and the US map array. Again, the idea of creating art with numbers and math hit me. But now I had 100 times the computing power, a rich language like ActionScript *and* the ability to put my creations on the web where they could be seen around the world. Yes, I was hooked.

There were still some things in Flash 5 that I was disappointed with. One of the major ones was the ability to draw graphics on the fly. Any graphic element had to be pre-drawn and then attached or duplicated onto the screen. Of course, these limitations led to some amazingly creative workarounds. There is the 100x100 diagonal line movie clip trick, which I consider one of the most elegant things I've ever discovered in Flash. One time there was a little impromptu competition at www.were-here.com, to create an animation using only a 1x1 square pixel and 50 lines or less of code. Using ActionScript to stretch, rotate and color that pixel, some absolutely amazing movies were made. But even with all this creativity, there were still things you just couldn't accomplish.

Then came Flash MX and the new drawing API. The ability to create an empty movie clip on the fly! moveTo, lineTo, beginFill, beginGradientFill! When I saw these commands, I was in heaven!

Altered vista

With all that in mind, I wanted to share some fun stuff with the drawing API. I figured that in order to show off the real differences between Flash 5 and Flash MX, I'd have to do something that would be virtually impossible in Flash 5. Note the use of the word "virtually". I've grown cautious of saying *anything* is impossible in *any* version of Flash! But with that disclaimer in mind, one thing you couldn't do easily in Flash 5 was filling a shape. Yes, I got pretty adept at scaling my 100x100 diagonal lines to make various dynamic shapes, but since each line was a separate movie clip, I never figured out how to fill the interior of that shape with a color. But now, it's a snap.

We're going to make a series of undulating movie clips that vary in shape, position and color, to create a virtual landscape.

First let's just get the hang of some of the new tools and make a wavy line.

The commands we'll be initially using are `moveTo(x, y)` and `lineTo(x, y)`. You can think of the line drawing tools as having a virtual pencil. Both of these commands move the pencil to a certain point on the stage, specified by the x and y arguments. `moveTo` is like lifting the pencil up and moving it, `lineTo` is like dragging the pencil from where it is to the new location, leaving a trail. If you don't specify an initial x, y, and use `lineTo` immediately, the line will be drawn from 0, 0. Also, after you draw a line, the pencil will stay where you left it, so if you then draw another line, it will be drawn from that point.

Now we could just issue these commands as is, and draw directly on the stage, or in `_root`. But since we will be making several shapes and positioning them, we'll draw each shape in its own movie clip. Here's another of my favorite features of MX: `createEmptyMovieClip`!

To create an empty movie clip, we merely need to give it a name and a depth. Add this to frame one of the main timeline.

```
createEmptyMovieClip("clip_mc", 0);
```

Now we have an empty movie clip named 'clip' on the stage. You should know that a new movie clip created this way will be located at 0, 0, or the upper left corner of the stage, you won't be able to see it though - there's nothing in it! Let's move it down to the middle of the stage so we can see it when we draw in it. We can keep it on the left edge though, since we'll be drawing left to right.

```
clip_mc._y = 200;
```

Next to define a line style, this is done, surprisingly enough, with the `lineStyle` command. This takes three arguments. The thickness of the line, the color, and its alpha or transparency. We'll make a one pixel black line, 100% opaque.

```
clip_mc.lineStyle(1, 0x000000, 100);
```

A quick note on colors. Any number beginning with 0x is a *hexadecimal* number (also called simply "hex"). Instead of going from 0 to 9, the digits in hex go from 0 to F, A-F standing for 10-15.

0	1	2	3	4	5	6	7	8	9	A	B	C	D	E	F
0	1	2	3	4	5	6	7	8	9	10	11	12	13	14	15

When you get into double digits, the left hand digit stands for "16's", just like in the decimal system it would stand for "10's". Therefore, in hex, 0x10 (remember the 0x prefix) is 16 decimal. 0xCA would be 218 decimal. (C=12. 12x16=208. A=10. 208+10=218)

Thus the numbers from 0-FF in hex are 0-255 in decimal. These are, coincidentally, the valid values for the color components red, green and blue. When you see a hex value as a color, with six digits after the 0X, the first two digits are the red values, the second two are green and last two are blue. Thus 0xFF0000 is red – it has a value of 255 for red, and 0 for green and blue. Note, that 0x000000 is simply 0, which is black. I usually simply use 0 if I am specifying black as a color.

Now we can start drawing. We don't need to do a moveTo since we'll start out at 0, 0 anyway. Remember, that's a 0, 0 as seen from the clip's coordinates, not the main stage. Since the clip is now at 0, 200, that's where the line will appear. We'll start out with a single horizontal line.

```
clip_mc.lineTo(550, 0);
```

You can go ahead and test what we've done so far and make sure it works for you.

Cool, but a single line doesn't give too much room for creativity. Let's break it up into a bunch of short lines. We'll replace the above line with a for loop to continuously increase the end point of the new line until it reaches the far end of the stage. Here's the whole thing:

```
createEmptyMovieClip("clip_mc", 0);
clip_mc._y = 200;
clip_mc.lineStyle(1, 0x000000, 100);
for (i=0; i<56; i++) {
    x = i*10;
    clip_mc.lineTo(x, y);
}
```

Here, the variable **i** will go from 0 to 55, giving us an **x** of 0 to 550. This doesn't look any different yet, but next we'll start messing around with the **y** values.

Here we'll just add in a y value somewhere between -10 and +10. This just makes a jagged line so we can see the individual segments – just so we know we're heading in the right direction.

```
for (i=0; i<56; i++) {
    x = i*10;
    y = Math.random()*20-10;
    clip_mc.lineTo(x, y);
```

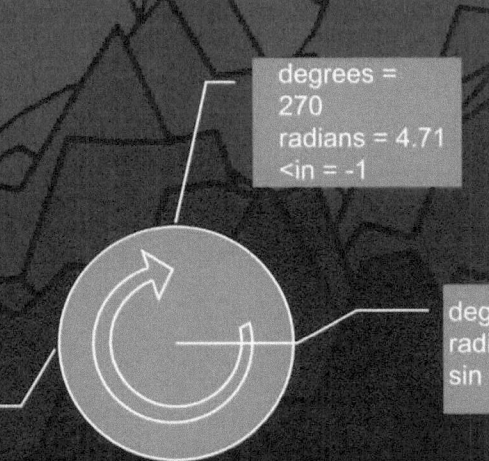

Now let's make it a bit smoother. The best way to make a smooth wave is with the trigonometric function, **sin**. Without getting into a big explanation of trig, this function is used like this:

```
variable = Math.sin(angle);
```

This will return a number from -1 to +1 as the angle goes around in a full circle.

The argument `angle` must be in radians, not degrees. One radian is about 59 degrees. You can convert them by using:

```
radians = degrees*PI/180;
degrees = radians*180/PI;
```

But for our purposes, we won't bother. We'll just use radians. A full circle is 2*PI radians, or about 6.28. So, as angle starts out at 0, `Math.sin(angle)` will return 0. As it gets to one quarter of the way through the circle, or about 1.57 radians, it will return 1. As it hits 3.14 radians, half way through the circle, it's back to 0, then goes through -1 then back to 0 again as it arrives at 6.28 and starts over.

Now we can easily multiply this return factor by any number we want to get a larger range. For example, if we multiply it by 20, we will get a wave going from -20 to 20. This multiplication factor will be the amplitude or height of the wave.

How fast we increase the angle will determine how fast it goes through the circle, and how quickly the resulting wave will go up and down. This is the wavelength.
So our `for` loop becomes this:

degrees = 270
radians = 4.71
<in = -1

degrees = 0
radians = 1.57
sin = 0

degrees = 1
80
radians = 3.14
<in = n

degrees = 9
0
radians = 1.57
<in = 1

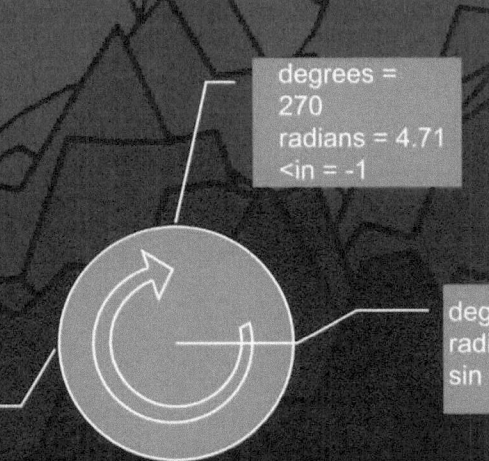

```
for (i=0; i<56; i++) {
    x = i*10;
    y = Math.sin(angleX += .3)*20;
    clip_mc.lineTo(x, y);
}
```

There we have it, a nifty little sine wave snaking across the screen. The value of .3 is added to `angleX` on each frame. This moves the sin through –1 to 1, multiplied by 20 gives us a wave from –20 to 20. Go ahead and change the .3 to some different values, as well as the 20, and see what different waves you wind up with.

Now, let's close it up and color it in. The following lines, right at the end of the file, will turn the single line into a closed shape:

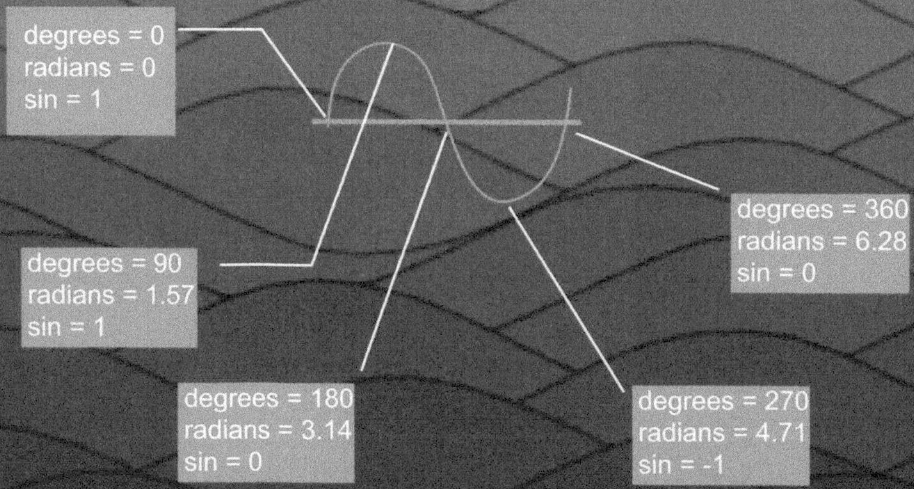

degrees = 0
radians = 0
sin = 1

degrees = 360
radians = 6.28
sin = 0

degrees = 90
radians = 1.57
sin = 1

degrees = 180
radians = 3.14
sin = 0

degrees = 270
radians = 4.71
sin = -1

```
clip_mc.lineTo(x, 50);
clip_mc.lineTo(0, 50);
clip_mc.lineTo(0, 0);
```

Now we color it in. This next bit is the part that was most impossible in Flash 5, but is only two lines of code in Flash MX! We simply tell Flash when to begin the fill, what color and alpha, and when to end the fill, using the two commands:

```
beginFill(color, alpha);
endFill();
```

The beginFill should go before you start drawing the lines – preferably right after you define your line style, and the end fill when you are done drawing lines. Color and alpha work the same way as with lineStyle. So let's fill it with a nice orange color. Here's our full code so far:

```
createEmptyMovieClip("clip_mc", 0);
clip_mc._y = 200;
clip_mc.lineStyle(1, 0x000000, 100);
clip_mc.beginFill(0xFF7700, 100);
for (i=0; i<56; i++) {
    x = i*10;
    y = Math.sin(angleX += .3)*20;
    clip_mc.lineTo(x, y);
}
clip_mc.lineTo(x, 50);
clip_mc.lineTo(0, 50);
clip_mc.lineTo(0, 0);
clip_mc.endFill();
```

OK, that about does it for making one shape, and that's about all we need to know about the drawing API for this file. All we're going to do now is make a whole bunch of these shapes and stack them up one behind the other.

First we turn the previous code into a function which we assign as an onEnterFrame handler to
_root

```
clipDepth = 0;
_root.onEnterFrame = drawShape;
function drawShape() {
  clip_mc = createEmptyMovieClip("clip"+clipDepth, 1000- clipDepth++);
  clipY = 400-clipDepth*10;
  if (clipY<=0) {
    delete _root.onEnterFrame;
  }
  clip_mc._y = clipY;
  clip_mc.lineStyle(1, 0x000000, 100);
  clip_mc.beginFill(0xFF7700, 100);
  angleX = 0;
  for (i=0; i<56; i++) {
    x = i*10;
    y = Math.sin(angleX += .3)*20;
    clip_mc.lineTo(x, y);
  }
  clip_mc.lineTo(x, 50);
  clip_mc.lineTo(0, 50);
  clip_mc.lineTo(0, 0);
  clip_mc.endFill();
}
```

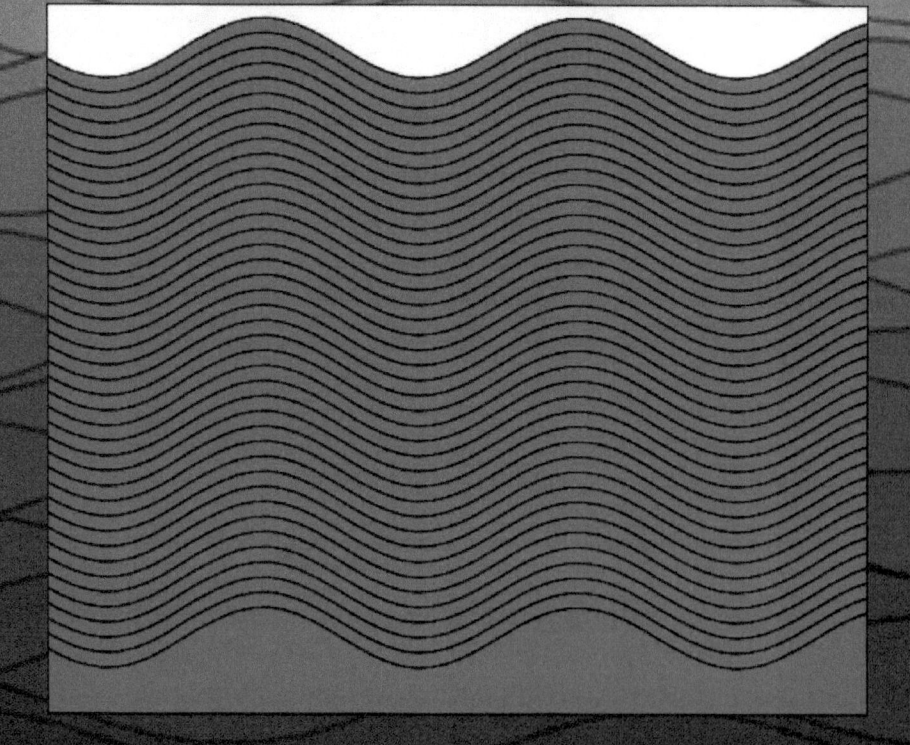

This might need a few points of explanation. First we assign the function `drawShape` as our `onEnterFrame` handler for `_root`, so it is executed once each frame. Then in the function itself we create our empty movie clip and assign it to a temporary variable `clip_mc`. The movie clip itself will have a dynamically generated name, because each clip will need a different name. We do this by adding the variable `clipDepth` to the string `clip`. We then assign a depth to the clip of `1000- clipDepth`. This has each successive clip assigned a lower depth, which puts it behind the last one. Also note we automatically increment `clipDepth` at the end.

We then set a variable named `clipY`, which is used to set the clip's `_y` property. This will start out at 400 and subtract 10 each time the function is run. If it becomes zero or less, then we have reached the top of the screen, so we can delete the `onEnterFrame` handler and be done with it.

The last change is the line which sets `angleX` back to 0 for each new clip.

You can test that and see the landscape begin to take shape.

Landscape painting

We now have the basic structure of the file down. From here on in, we are just making it more interesting. First thing you notice is that the waves are all lined up perfectly in rows, which is pretty boring. That's because we reset angleX to zero on each loop. Well, heck, let's throw a wave in there too! In the same way we set a wave using Math.sin for the wave height, we can put a wave on the horizontal position of the wave by varying what angleX starts with. This is probably more easily seen than explained. We change the angleX definition to:

```
angleX = Math.sin(angleY+=.24)*3;
```

Hey! Now we're getting somewhere! Now, you might be asking where I got those numbers - .24 and 3. Again, those are the wavelength and amplitude of the side-to-side wave we just created. The number you add to angleY determines how fast the wave will go back and forth. The number you multiply the result by will determine how far back and forth it goes. The numbers I used were just ones I got after playing around with until it started to look right. Bear in mind that I may look like a genius because I'm explaining all this so matter-of-factly. You don't see the hours of trial and error that went into it! Anyway, the wave is easier to see in action. To make it a bit easier for you to play around with, I've replaced all the hard-coded values with variables:

```
ampX = 20;
wavelengthX = .3;
ampY = 3;
wavelengthY = .24;
clipDepth = 0;
_root.onEnterFrame = drawShape;
function drawShape() {
    clip_mc = createEmptyMovieClip("clip"+ clipDepth, 1000- clipDepth++);
    clipY = 400- clipDepth*10;
    if (clipY<0) {
      delete _root.onEnterFrame;
    }
    clip_mc._y = clipY;
    clip_mc.lineStyle(1, 0x000000, 100);
    clip_mc.beginFill(0xFF7700, 100);
    angleX = Math.sin(angleY += wavelengthY)*ampY;
    for (i=0; i<56; i++) {
      x = i*10;
      y = Math.sin(angleX += wavelengthX)*ampX;
      clip_mc.lineTo(x, y);
    }
    clip_mc.lineTo(x, 50);
    clip_mc.lineTo(0, 50);
    clip_mc.lineTo(0, 0);
    clip_mc.endFill ();
}
```

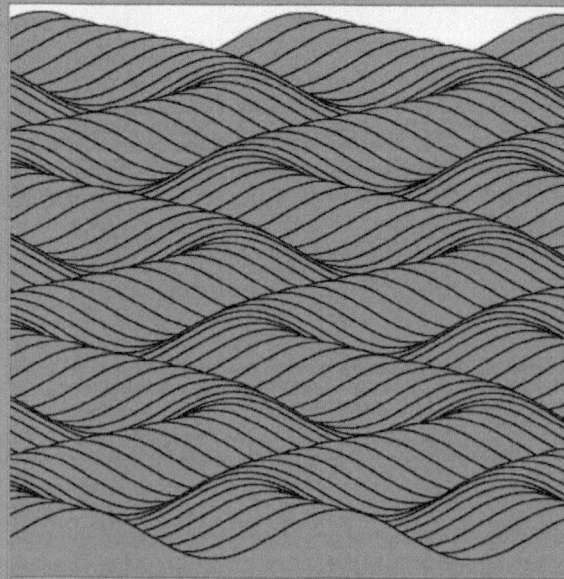

Now let's jack up the fascination factor by throwing another wave into the mix. This will go right alongside our angleX but will be a lower amplitude and higher wavelength. It will serve to make the existing wave a little "bumpy". We'll call this angleX1. We'll also need a amplitude, ampX1, and a wavelength, wavelengthX1. When we create our y value, we'll add both of these waves into it:

```
y = Math.sin(angleX += wavelengthX)*ampX + Math.sin(angleX1 += wavelengthX1)*ampX1;
```

Here's the final code:

```
ampX = 20;
wavelengthX = .3;
ampX1 = 3;
wavelengthX1 = 1.5;
ampY = 3;
wavelengthY = .24;
clipDepth = 0;
_root.onEnterFrame = drawShape;
function drawShape() {
    clip_mc = createEmptyMovieClip("clip"+ clipDepth, 1000- clipDepth++);
    clipY = 400-clipDepth*10;
    if (clipY<0) {
      delete _root.onEnterFrame;
    }
    clip_mc._y = clipY;
    clip_mc.lineStyle(1, 0x000000, 100);
    clip_mc.beginFill(0xFF7700, 100);
    angleX = Math.sin(angleY += wavelengthY)*ampY;
    for (i=0; i<56; i++) {
      x = i*10;
      y = Math.sin(angleX += wavelengthX)*ampX
      +Math.sin(angleX1 += wavelengthX1)*ampX1;
      clip_mc.lineTo(x, y);
    }
    clip_mc.lineTo(x, 50);
    clip_mc.lineTo(0, 50);
    clip_mc.lineTo(0, 0);
    clip_mc.endFill();
}
```

By playing around with that, you can add all sorts of textures to your evolving landscape. I should also mention that if you want to get a slightly higher resolution, you can change the line that says:

```
    clipY = 400-clipDepth*10;
```

to:

```
    clipY = 400-clipDepth*5;
```

This will put each successive clip a little closer to the last, and make more of them in total.

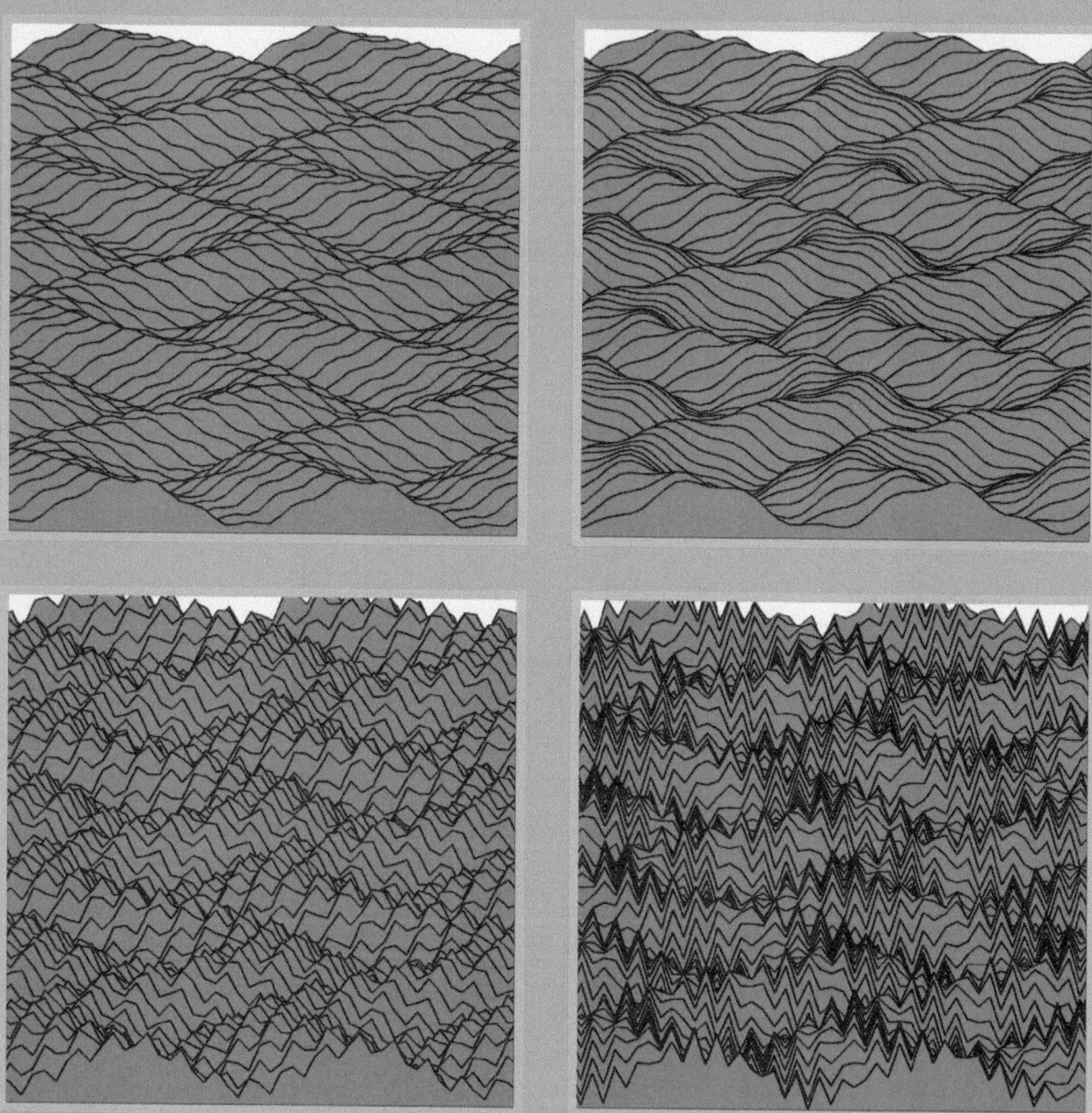

Now, if you've been following along exactly, typing each line exactly as written ... then I bet you are pretty sick of orange hills right about now. Let's throw in some color gradients. You may be aware of the `beginGradientFill` command in the drawing API of Flash MX, but we aren't even going to get into that just yet. We'll just use the color settings in `beginFill` but vary them for each new clip, the same way we are varying the angles.

First, we need to set up six values. These will be the beginning (bottom) and end (top) values for the red, green and blue components of our color fill. Each one of them can be anything from 0 to 255. These will be decided right up at the top of the file. Here's what I chose:

```
r1 = 160;
g1 = 128;
b1 = 32;
r2 = 0;
g2 = 255;
b2 = 96;
```

Right after that, we need to find the difference between the two and divide that by how many shapes we will actually draw. For what we've done so far, we wind up with 40 individual shapes (we start at _y = 400 and subtract 10 until it's 0. 400/10=40).

```
rinc = (r2-r1)/40;
ginc = (g2-g1)/40;
binc = (b2-b1)/40;
```

This gives us the amount we have to increment each color value each frame/new shape, to go from the beginning color to the end. Remember if you change any of the factors that we used to calculate the 40 with, you'll have to change that number. For example, if you only subtracted 5 from _y each frame, you'd wind up with 80 shapes, so you'd use the 80 instead of 40.

Then, just before our `beginFill` line, we need to combine the three color components into a color that Flash can use. Here I'll show you one of my favorite neat little tricks for working with color. It involves bitwise shift operators (`<<`) and the bitwise OR operator (`|`)which is the vertical line, often called the "pipe" usually right on the same key as \ on most keyboards). If you want more info on how these work, check the ActionScript Dictionary. Basically, we are using some fancy, but very concise code to combine the three component colors into one large 24-bit number representing a color value. Here's the line:

```
shapeCol = r1 << 16 | g1 << 8 | b1;
```

Now we just use that variable, `shapeCol` in our `beginFill` command:

```
clip.beginFill(shapeCol, 100);
```

Here's what we have so far:

```
r1 = 160;
g1 = 128;
b1 = 32;
r2 = 0;
g2 = 255;
b2 = 96;
rinc = (r2-r1)/40;
ginc = (g2-g1)/40;
binc = (b2-b1)/40;
ampX = 20;
wavelengthX = .3;
ampX1 = 3;
wavelengthX1 = 1.5;
ampY = 3;
wavelengthY = .24;
clipDepth = 0;
_root.onEnterFrame = drawShape;
function drawShape() {
    clip_mc = createEmptyMovieClip("clip"+ clipDepth, 1000- clipDepth++);
    clipY = 400-clipDepth*10;
    if (clipY<0) {
      delete _root.onEnterFrame;
    }
    clip_mc._y = clipY;
    clip_mc.lineStyle(1, 0x000000, 100);
    shapeCol = r1 << 16 | g1 << 8 | b1;
    clip_mc.beginFill(shapeCol, 100);
    angleX = Math.sin(angleY += wavelengthY)*ampY;
    for (i=0; i<56; i++) {
      x = i*10;
      y = Math.sin(angleX += wavelengthX)*ampX
      +Math.sin(angleX1 += wavelengthX1)*ampX1;
      clip_mc.lineTo(x, y);
    }
    clip_mc.lineTo(x, 50);
    clip_mc.lineTo(0, 50);
    clip_mc.lineTo(0, 0);
    clip_mc.endFill();
}
```

The final thing left is to add the increment values to the color component values, so that next time around the colors will be slightly different. This will be done at the end of the drawShape() function, so the values get updated each frame.

```
r1 += rinc;
g1 += ginc;
b1 += binc;
```

One small thing I noticed at this point was the line defining the shape seemed a bit too harsh, giving it a cartoon feel. I just changed the `lineStyle` line to reduce the alpha down to about 20 and that gave it a much subtler effect. Here's the final code up to now:

```
r1 = 160;
g1 = 128;
b1 = 32;
r2 = 0;
g2 = 255;
b2 = 96;
rinc = (r2-r1)/40;
ginc = (g2-g1)/40;
binc = (b2-b1)/40;
ampX = 20;
wavelengthX = .3;
ampX1 = 3;
wavelengthX1 = 1.5;
ampY = 3;
wavelengthY = .24;
clipDepth = 0;
_root.onEnterFrame = drawShape;
function drawShape() {
    clip_mc = createEmptyMovieClip("clip"+ clipDepth, 1000- clipDepth++);
    clipY = 400-clipDepth*10;
    if (clipY<0) {
        delete _root.onEnterFrame;
    }
    clip_mc._y = clipY;
    clip_mc.lineStyle(1, 0x000000, 20);
    shapeCol = r1 << 16 | g1 << 8 | b1;
    clip_mc.beginFill(shapeCol, 100);
    angleX = Math.sin(angleY += wavelengthY)*ampY;
    for (i=0; i<56; i++) {
        x = i*10;
        y = Math.sin(angleX += wavelengthX)*ampX
        +Math.sin(angleX1 += wavelengthX1)*ampX1;
        clip_mc.lineTo(x, y);
    }
    clip_mc.lineTo(x, 50);
    clip_mc.lineTo(0, 50);
    clip_mc.lineTo(0, 0);
    clip_mc.endFill();
    r1 += rinc;
    g1 += ginc;
```

Lastly, just to easily explore the infinite possibilities, I assigned random numbers to all of the initialization values. I threw the whole first block of code in an init() function, and set that function as the onMouseDown handler. Now each time you click the mouse, you draw a new landscape. This kind of thing keeps me busy for hours (OK, I'm strange!). Here's what that looks like:

```
onMouseDown = init;
function init() {
    r1 = Math.random()*128;
    g1 = Math.random()*128;
    b1 = Math.random()*128;
    r2 = Math.random()*128+127;
    g2 = Math.random()*128+127;
    b2 = Math.random()*128+127;
    rinc = (r2-r1)/40;
    ginc = (g2-g1)/40;
    binc = (b2-b1)/40;
    ampX = Math.random()*20+5;
    wavelengthX = Math.random();
    ampX1 = Math.random()*10;
    wavelengthX1 = Math.random()*3;
    ampY = Math.random()*10;
    wavelengthY = Math.random();
    clipDepth = 0;
    _root.onEnterFrame = drawShape;
}
```

This is simply followed by the existing drawShape function.

Run this full screen, do a screen capture and save it as a picture file – it makes some cool wallpaper!

My final version can be downloaded from www.friendsofED.com as project_01.fla.

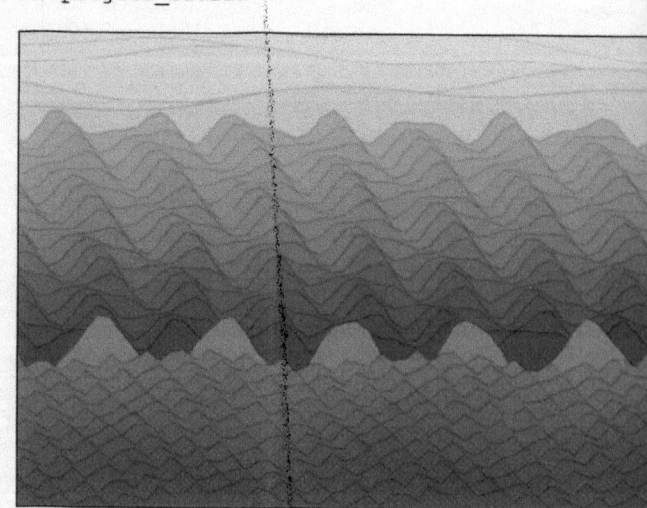

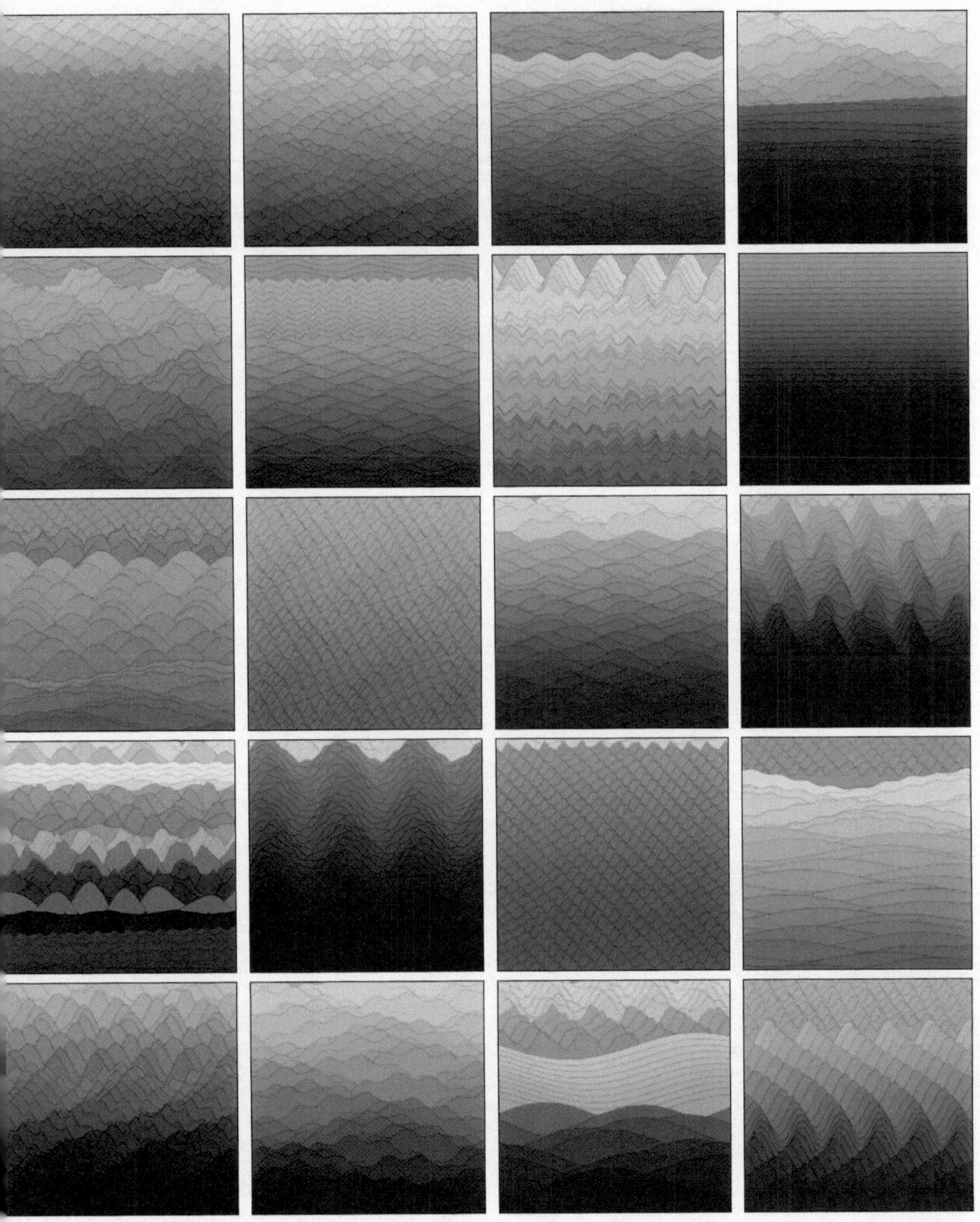

Curving

The next function I wanted to check in on is curveTo. As exciting as lineTo is, as you can see, it can take a lot of work to make a simple curve. Luckily our friends at Macromedia threw in this command for us to play with.

curveTo works a lot like lineTo. It starts wherever the pen happens to be located and draws a line to the coordinates you give it. However, you must specify an additional two parameters, which make up a control point which tell the curve how to curve.

As they say, a picture is worth a thousand words, and a SWF has got to be worth several times more than that. We'll specify two points, x1, y1 and x2, y2 and draw a curve between them. For the control point, we'll use the mouse pointer (_xmouse, _ymouse). In a new FLA, start with this code in the first frame:

```
x1 = 100;
y1 = 200;
x2 = 450;
y2 = 200;
onEnterFrame = function () {
    _root.clear();
    _root.lineStyle(1, 0, 100);
    _root.moveTo(x1, y1);
    _root.curveTo(_xmouse, _ymouse, x2, y2);
};
```

That was pretty simple. Now I know my first reaction when I first created this was, "Hey, the curve isn't *touching* the mouse! That's not too useful." So, I'm guessing you might be thinking the same thing. The control point is where the curve goes *toward*, but is not meant to hit there. Of course, it would be a lot more useful in many cases if you could dictate exactly where the curve landed. But how?

I wasn't the only one with that question. It started popping up around the web and the answer I got came from Robert Penner. If we call the point we want to hit as targetX, targetY, and the point we feed to curveTo is controlX, controlY, here's the formula:

```
controlX = targetX*2-(x1+x2)/2;
controlY = targetY*2-(y1+y2)/2;
```

Now, if I understood that in a lot more depth, I would doubt explain how it works in a lot more detail. What I know is that it does work, and it's pretty simple to remember. Now let's see it in action. We'll just apply that formula using the mouse position as a target. We'll compute the control point and feed that into curve to. Try this:

```
x1 = 100;
y1 = 200;
x2 = 450;
y2 = 200;
onEnterFrame = function () {
    controlX = _xmouse*2-(x1+x2)/2;
    controlY = _ymouse*2-(y1+y2)/2;
    _root.clear();
    _root.lineStyle(1, 0, 100);
    _root.moveTo(x1, y1);
    _root.curveTo(controlX, controlY, x2, y2);
};
```

Jello ball

Now that we have the basics down, let's move on to the ne major project. This is a re-creation of one of the first files did when I got a hold of Flash MX. I was excited about th possibilities of using curveTo to make dynamic, organ shapes. I feel like this project really captured what I wante to do with it. Basically, we'll be using a series of curveTo's create a circle. Then, by manipulating the points that make u the curves, with a little springiness thrown in, we'll have a b blob of jiggling jello on our screen. Don't worry though, washes off easily.

First we will need a bunch of points and a way of storin them. There are a number of ways of doing this. I chose t use objects. An object is simply a piece of data stored memory. But unlike a simple variable, an object can contai additional variables, called properties or members, and ca even contain its own functions, usually called methods. T begin with, our objects will just have two properties, x and Later we'll add a few more, and the object will neatly pack age up all the data we need for each point.

There are two main ways of creating an object. One is to us the new keyword and say:

```
point = new Object();
```

ou can then go along and create its properties:

```
point.x = 275;
point.y = 200;
```

etc.

he alternate way is a bit of a shortcut that lets you create our object and its properties and even assign values to them ll at once. You simply list your properties in curly braces. Use colon after each property to specify its value, and separate ach property/value pair with a comma:

```
point = {x: 275, y: 200};
```

Ve're going to make a set of 20 point objects and rather than ssigning each to a variable, we'll store them in an array. This nakes it very easy to handle them sequentially in a loop. In act we'll use a loop to fill the array in the first place. Here's ur code to begin with:

```
MAX = 20;
points_array = new Array();
for (i=0; i<max; i++) {
    points_array[i] = {x:275, y:200};
}
```

Ve just created a new array called points_array, and ooped through it 20 times, filling each element with a new bject. Each object has an x and y property, set to 275 and 00, center stage.

o far so good, but so what? We need the points arranged in circle to begin with, not clumped together in the middle of he screen. We will space the points out evenly around the ircle. So we'll need to slice our circle up like a pie. We need o know how big each slice is (what its angle is).

Ve already decided on 20 points, which makes 20 slices. A ircle is 360 degrees, so 360/20 is 18 degrees each. Cool, but emember that Flash likes radians, not degrees. We could fig- re it in degrees and then convert, but that eats up a lot of verhead, and we may need all the CPU cycles we can spare nce we start plugging in the formulas below. So if you can rit your teeth and deal with radians just a bit more, it'll pay ff. It's good practice anyway!

OK, as we covered earlier, a circle is PI*2 radians, so one slice is Math.PI*2/20. Don't even worry what that number turns out to be. You don't need to know it or ever even see it. We'll just stick it in a variable and be done with it.

```
oneSlice = Math.PI*2/max;
```

There we go. Remember that max was already set to 20, so we'll use that. If we later decide we want more or less points, we just change the value of max, and everything will be recalculated and work just fine.

The last thing we need to decide before we plot our points is how big the circle will be. How's 200 pixels sound? OK. So its radius will be 100. We'll just define that at the start:

```
radius = 100;
```

Now we can jump back into the FOR loop and get some real values for each point's x and y. For this we use some basic trigonometry. You survived through it last time, so be brave. First off, we'll determine the actual angle of the current point. We know what oneSlice is, and the variable i, keeps track of the number of times through the loop, or how many slices there are. So the current angle will be i times oneSlice.

```
angle = oneSlice*i;
```

Now here's the trig part. These are the formulas for getting the x and y values of a point when you know its radius and angle:

```
xPosition = cos(angle) * radius
yPosition = sin(angle) * radius
```

Now that will give you the position in relation to the center of the circle. We'll have to add something that to align the center of the circle with the center of the screen. Here are those formulas fit into our current file so far:

```
MAX = 20;
oneSlice = Math.PI*2/max;
radius = 100;
points_array = new Array();
for (i=0; i<max; i++) {
    angle = oneSlice*i;
    xPos = Math.cos(angle)*radius+275;
    yPos = Math.sin(angle)*radius+200;
    points_array[i] = {x:xPos, y:yPos};
}
```

Now, you can go ahead and test that if you want, but you're not going to see much. Remember that an object is just a collection of data. It doesn't have any visual representation on the screen, unlike a movie clip, which usually contains graphic content. We need to take those x and y values and feed them to some drawing API command to see what we've created.

We'll start with the lineTo command we already know. We just do a moveTo to the first point, then loop through the array, drawing lines to each successive point, starting at point 1. When we finish the array, we draw one final line back to point 0 and close up the circle. Just type this in after all the last piece of code:

```
_root.lineStyle(1, 0, 100);
_root.moveTo(points_array[0].x, points_array[0].y);
for (i=1; i<max; i++) {
    _root.lineTo(points_array[i].x, points_array[i].y);
}
_root.lineTo(points_array[0].x, points_array[0].y);
```

Test that to see the circle come into being.

Now let's alter it to use curveTo. We'll start out the same, moving to point 0 and starting a for loop. But since curveTo takes four parameters, representing two points, we need to increment our counter by 2 each loop. We'll basically be using one point as the control point, and the next point as the end point of the curve.

We also need to change the test portion of the for statement to read i<max-1, so that in our final curve we have one point left over as a control point when we loop back to point 0. This code should be pretty self explanatory if you've followed everything so far:

```
MAX = 20;
oneSlice = Math.PI*2/max;
radius = 100;
points_array = new Array();
for (i=0; i<max; i++) {
    angle = oneSlice*i;
    xPos = Math.cos(angle)*radius+275;
    yPos = Math.sin(angle)*radius+200;
    points_array[i] = {x:xPos, y:yPos};
}
_root.lineStyle(1, 0, 100);
_root.moveTo(points_array[0].x, points_array[0].y);
for (i=1; i<max-1; i += 2) {
    _root.curveTo(points_array[i].x, points_array[i].y, points_array[i+1].x,
points_array[i+1].y);
}
_root.curveTo(points_array[i].x, points_array[i].y, points_array[0].x,
points_array[0].y);
```

This draws a somewhat smoother circle. Not perfect, but smooth enough for our purposes. We could use the trick from above – of placing the curve directly on the target point. That would create a near perfect circle. But again, that would also eat up a lot more processor time. So this somewhat lumpy circle will suffice!

Next up, we will throw in some springiness and really bring the circle to life.

For something to spring, we need a few more pieces of information:

A target – where is it moving *to*?   `xTarget, yTarget`
Velocity – how fast is it going, and in what direction?   `xVelocity, yVelocity`
Springiness – how much does it bounce?   `SPRING`
Damping – how soon will it come to rest?   `DAMP`

Each of our 20 points will be independently springing around. Therefore each will need its own target and its own individual velocity. Both of these factors will be broken down into x and y factors, giving us an xTarget, yTarget, xVelocity, yVelocity. In addition, each point will have its own springiness factor, so each will behave slightly differently. This will simply be defined as *spring*. These will become five additional properties that we will define when creating each object. So, going back to where we create the point objects, the line becomes:

```
points[i] = {x:275, y:200, xTarget:275, yTarget:200,
xVelocity:0, yVelocity:0, spring:Math.random()*.5+.5};
```

Here we reverted back to having x and y initialize center screen. We also used those values for the target, and set the velocities to zero. Spring was set to a random number between .5 and 1.0.

Now we jump up to the top of the file and throw in a damping factor. This will be a global factor, the same for all points. Here's the first part of the file (I temporarily removed the drawing part):

```
DAMP = .9;
MAX = 20;
oneSlice = Math.PI*2/max;
radius = 100;
points_array = new Array();
for (i=0; i<max; i++) {
    points_array[i] = {x:275, y:200, xTarget:275, yTarget:200,
    xVelocity:0, yVelocity:0, spring:Math.random()*.5+.5};
}
```

Now we have all the pieces in place, it's time to animate them. The way a spring works is that an object is attracted to a target point. The further away from the point it is, the stronger the attraction. Imagine snapping a rubber band. The further you pull it, the more power it snaps with. This force pulling it towards the target can be called acceleration. Acceleration essentially changes and object's velocity. The acceleration in a spring is proportional to the distance from the object to the target.

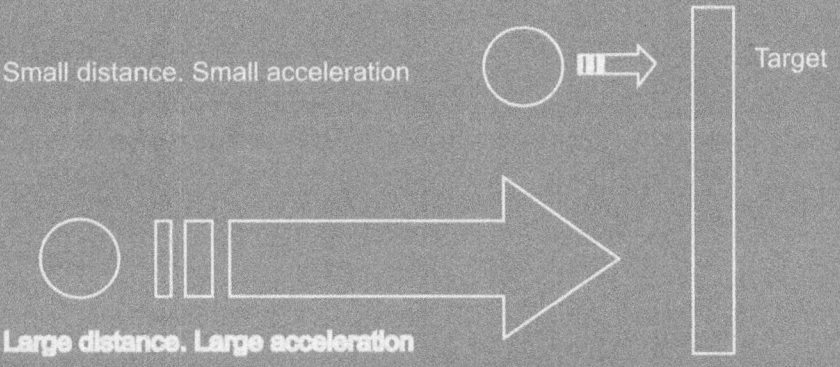

Small distance. Small acceleration

Target

Large distance. Large acceleration

So, the next thing we need to do is determine the point's target x and y. This will be the same code we used earlier to simply space the points in a circle, except we will use the mouse coordinates as a center point. Thus, the points will be *trying* to form a circle around the mouse cursor. We want this to be updated as the mouse moves, so we stick it in an onEnterFrame function:

```
_root.onEnterFrame = function () {
  for (i=0; i<max; i++) {
    angle = oneSlice*i;
    point = points_array[i];
    point.xTarget = Math.cos(angle)*radius+ _xmouse;
    point.yTarget = Math.sin(angle)*radius+ _ymouse;
  }
};
```

This should all look pretty similar. We just created a temporary variable, point, to use as we calculate the various properties. It's just easier to type "point" than "points_array[i]" over and over – and it is also executes faster in Flash!

Now that we've calculated the xTarget and yTarget for each point, we need to find the distance between the current value of each point and its target. Then we multiply this by the spring factor to come up with an acceleration for that point. This sounds harder than it looks. This code goes right in the for loop after we define the targets:

```
accelX = (point.xTarget-point.x)*point.spring;
accelY = (point.yTarget-point.y)*point.spring;
```

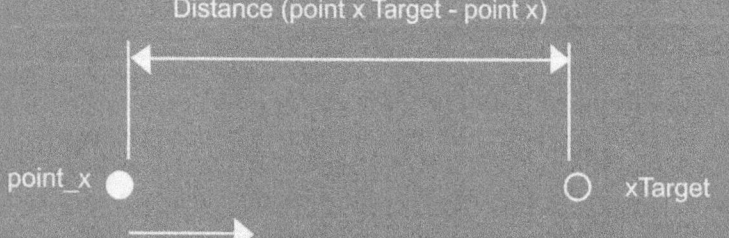

Distance (point x Target - point x)

point_x   ○ xTarget

accelX will be a fraction of the distance from point to the target

We just subtract the current value from the target value and multiply times spring.

Now that we have the acceleration values, we simply add them to the point's current velocity. The next two lines are:

```
point.xVelocity += accelX;
point.yVelocity += accelY;
```

Here's what we have so far in our onEnterFrame function:

```
_root.onEnterFrame = function() {
  for (i=0; i<max; i++) {
    angle = oneSlice*i;
    point = points_array[i];
    point.xTarget = Math.cos(angle)*radius+ _xmouse;
    point.yTarget = Math.sin(angle)*radius+ _ymouse;
    accelX = (point.xTarget-point.x)*point.spring;
    accelY = (point.yTarget-point.y)*point.spring;
    point.xVelocity += accelX;
    point.yVelocity += accelY;
  }
};
```

This gives us the updated velocity with which the point will move. It is now time to throw in that damping factor. In the real world, nothing will bounce around forever. Even that ultra-mega-super-ball you bought as a kid eventually came to a rest – after freaking out the cat, knocking over your mom's vase and whacking Dad in the head. That's because as it moved and bounced, it was losing energy. If we don't take that into account, we won't have a jello ball, we'll have chaos.

To simulate the loss of energy, we just multiply each velocity factor by damp, which we've set at .9. Therefore, on each frame, the velocity becomes 90% of what it would have been, and eventually the points will slow down and come to a stop. Again, it's simpler when you see it:

```
point.xVelocity *= damp;
point.yVelocity *= damp;
```

Now we simply add the current velocity to the point's x and y values:

```
point.x += point.xVelocity;
point.y += point.yVelocity;
```

We're just about done. All we need to do now is close up that `for` loop and plug back in the drawing code we made before. Here's the final code:

```
DAMP = .9;
MAX = 20;
oneSlice = Math.PI*2/max;
radius = 100;
points_array = new Array();
for (i=0; i<max; i++) {
    points_array[i] = {x:275, y:200, xTarget:275, yTarget:200,
    ➥xVelocity:0, yVelocity:0, spring:Math.random()*.5+.5};
}
_root.onEnterFrame = function() {
   for (i=0; i<max; i++) {
     angle = oneSlice*i;
     point = points_array[i];
     point.xTarget = Math.cos(angle)*radius+_xmouse;
     point.yTarget = Math.sin(angle)*radius+_ymouse;
     accelX = (point.xTarget-point.x)*point.spring;
     accelY = (point.yTarget-point.y)*point.spring;
     point.xVelocity += accelX;
     point.yVelocity += accelY;
     point.xVelocity *= damp;
     point.yVelocity *= damp;
     point.x += point.xVelocity;
     point.y += point.yVelocity;
   }
   _root.clear();
   _root.lineStyle(1, 0, 100);
   _root.beginFill(0x00ff00, 100);
   _root.moveTo(points_array[0].x, points_array[0].y);
   for (i=1; i<max-1; i += 2) {
     _root.curveTo(points_array[i].x, points_array[i].y,
     ➥points_array[i+1].x, points_array[i+1].y);
   }
 _root.curveTo(points_array[i].x, points_array[i].y,
 ➥ points_array[0].x, points_array[0].y);
   _root.endFill();
};
```

Notice I also plugged in a `beginFill` and `endFill` statement there to give the ball some color. You now have a bouncing blob of green jello. Actually, when you first start it up, it may look more like a Picasso painting until it settles down a bit. Try messing around with some of the key variables – notably the `spring` definition and the `damp` variable, to control just how springy it is, and how quickly it quiets down. This file is `project_02.fla`, for download.

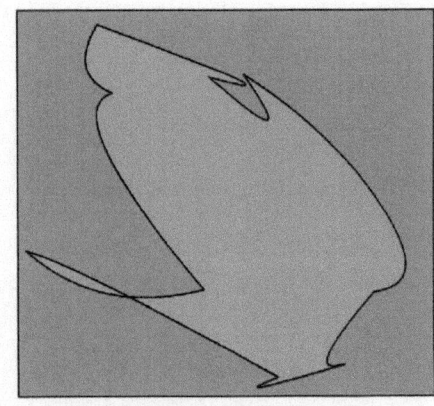

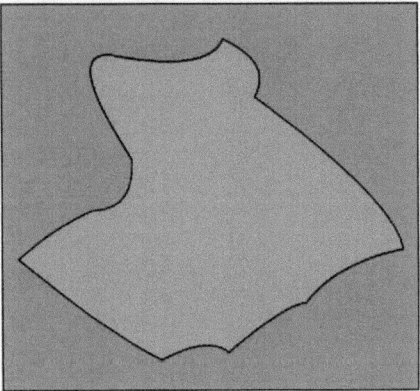

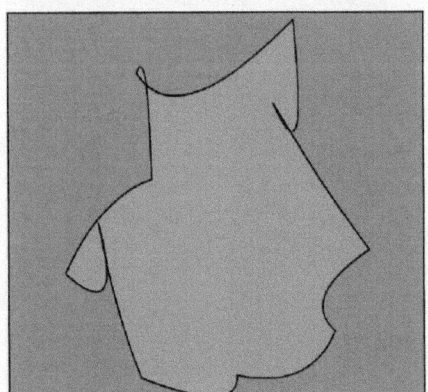

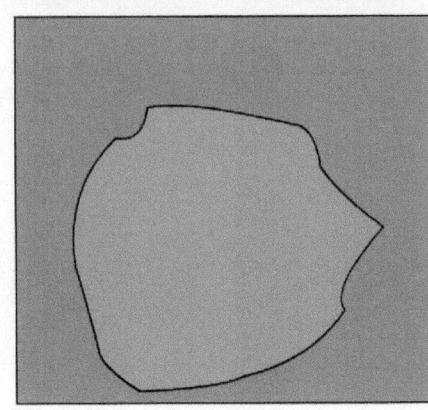

Gradients

The only thing we haven't hit upon in the drawing API yet is gradient fills. If everything else wasn't enough, this adds some real power to your ability to make stunning visual effects with Flash MX.

To create a gradient fill, we simply replace the command `beginFill` with `beginGradientFill`. OK, maybe my use of the word "simply" was a bit premature – in `beginFill` we merely had to specify a color and an alpha; with a gradient fill, we have to define we get to define the type of fill, the colors used, the alphas, the ratio of one color to the other(s), and the direction and size of the fill. Specifically, here is the syntax of the command:

```
beginGradientFill(fillType, colors, alphas,
ratios, matrix);
```

OK, let's take them one at a time...

- **fillType** – this is a string, which can be either radial or linear. A radial gradient will expand like a circle, with one color in the center and other colors radiating outward in rings. A linear fill goes from left to right, starting with one color and blending into any others as it goes.

- **colors** – this is an array, each element holding a color value. You can create an array using the new operator, and then fill it in:

```
col_array = new Array();
  col_array[0] = 0xff0000;
  col_array[1] = 0x0000ff;
```

...or you can use the shortcut method, similar to the object creation shortcut, just use square brackets, filling in each color value separated by commas:

```
col_array = [0xff0000, 0x0000ff];
```

You can define as many colors as you want for the array. If you just use two, it will blend from the first to the second. If you add more, you will get bands or rings of different colors.

- **alphas** – this is also an array. This array will contain values from 0 (fully transparent) to 100 (opaque). It is important to note that the colors, alphas and ratios arrays all must have exactly the same amount of element. You can't have two colors and three alphas. If you try, your gradient will fail silently, leaving you wondering what happened.

- **ratios** – another array. This accepts values from 0 to 255. These show where in the gradient each color starts. For a linear gradient, 0 is the far left and 255 is the far right of the gradient. If you have two colors and want them to blend evenly across the entire width, enter [0, 255]. If, for example, you entered [0, 128], the first color would blend completely into the second about half way across the gradient. Radials work the same way, but 0 is at the center and 255 at the outer edge.

- **matrix** – **not** an array this time, but an object. This object contains variables that control where the gradient starts, how big it is, and if it is rotated, how much so. Here is a typical object definition for a matrix:

```
matrix = {matrixType: "box", x: 0, y: 0,
➡ w: 100,h: 100, r: 0};
```

OK, lets go through those...

- matrixType is a string, "box". That's the only valid value for it.

- x and y are the coordinates where the gradient will begin.w and h are the width and height of the gradient.

- r is the rotation (in radians once again).

All right, enough explanations, let's put it to work and see it in action.

```
colors = [0xff0000, 0x0000ff];
alphas = [100, 100];
ratios = [0, 255];
matrix = {matrixType:"box", x:0, y:0, w:550,
➡ h:400, r:0};

_root.beginGradientFill("radial", colors,
➡ alphas, ratios, matrix);
```

```
_root.lineTo(550, 0);
_root.lineTo(550, 400);
_root.lineTo(0, 400);
_root.lineTo(0, 0);
_root.endFill();
```

We defined our colors, alphas, ratios and matrix, then plugged them into the beginGradientFill() statement, then just drew a simple box around the screen. Don't forget endFill(), which works the same whether your fill is plain or gradient.

This gives you a pretty gaudy red to blue circular gradient. Ugly, but effective at demonstrating what's going on. Now try changing the fillType parameter from "radial" to "linear". This shows you the linear gradient in action. Now, with "linear" still in place, change first three lines to:

```
colors = [0xff0000, 0x00ff00, 0x0000ff];
alphas = [100, 100, 100];
ratios = [0, 40, 255];
```

This shows you the effect of having three colors specified. Note that the green color is concentrated close to the left, because we put a value of 40 in ratios for the middle color. Try playing around with that to get the feel for it.

Now if it was just about setting up some numbers and creating a gradient that just sits there, that would be pretty boring. You may as well just use the gradient fill tool in the authoring environment – it's a lot more intuitive. When we use code to do things, we can change the numbers over time and start creating some really cool, dynamic effects, things you could never do with the authoring environment, and never in Flash 5 either!

Earlier we used Math.sin to create some waves. This is one of the most useful functions I have ever found. I use it for so many things – any time I want some value to cycle back and forth smoothly. If you combine a couple of sin statements with different parameters, you can get what looks like completely random, chaotic results. Even though it's just a couple of waves, each of which are very logical and easy to follow, the combination seems completely random. We'll be using that here.

What we will do is take a color value and break it down into its three separate components, red, green and blue. Each one of these can be a value from 0 to 255.

As we saw earlier, Math.sin() returns a value from -1 to +1. If we multiply that times 127, we get -127 to +127. If we add that to the value of 128, we get a result that loops back and forth from 1 to 255. Perfect! Now we can start.

Here is our code for one of those component colors:

```
redSpeed1 = .1;
_root.onEnterFrame = function () {
    redAngle1 += redSpeed1
    red1 = Math.sin(redAngle1)*127+128;
}
```

Here, we assign a value to redSpeed1 of .1, and then in an onEnterFrame function, we add that value to redAngle1. We then feed that to Math.sin. As we take the redAngle1 around in a circle, we'll get a result looping through 0, 1, 0, -1, 0, etc. Multiply the result by 127 and it will go up and down from -127 to +127. Add that to 128. This will result in red1 cycling from 1 to 255 continuously.

Now we just do the same thing with green and blue, using slightly different speeds:

```
redSpeed1 = .1;
greenSpeed1 = .07;
blueSpeed1 = .04;
_root.onEnterFrame = function () {
    redAngle1 += redSpeed1;
    greenAngle1 += greenSpeed1;
    blueAngle1 += blueSpeed1;
    red1 = Math.sin(redAngle1)*127+128;
    green1 = Math.sin(greenAngle1)*127+128;
    blue1 = Math.sin(blueAngle1)*127+128;
}
```

We now have a valid value for red, green and blue. As we covered earlier in the chapter, we can combine these into a value Flash can understand for color:

```
col1 = red1 << 16 | green1 << 8 | blue1;
```

OK, we are half way there. We have defined one cycling color. The good news is, the second color is just as easy, just copy everything above and change the 1s to 2s! I also picked some other different values for the speed variables.

```
redSpeed1 = .1;
greenSpeed1 = .07;
blueSpeed1 = .04;
redSpeed2 = .09;
greenSpeed2 = .06;
blueSpeed2 = .03;
_root.onEnterFrame = function () {
    redAngle1 += redSpeed1;
    greenAngle1 += greenSpeed1;
    blueAngle1 += blueSpeed1;
    redAngle2 += redSpeed2;
    greenAngle2 += greenSpeed2;
    blueAngle2 += blueSpeed2;
    red1 = Math.sin(redAngle1)*127+128;
    green1 = Math.sin(greenAngle1)*127+128;
    blue1 = Math.sin(blueAngle1)*127+128;
    red2 = Math.sin(redAngle2)*127+128;
    green2 = Math.sin(greenAngle2)*127+128;
    blue2 = Math.sin(blueAngle2)*127+128;
    col1 = red1 << 16 | green1 << 8 | blue1;
    col2 = red2 << 16 | green2 << 8 | blue2;
}
```

Now we have two color values, col1 and col2, which are composed of red green and blue components, which are constantly changing. We just need to plug these into a colors array and feed that into our beginGradientFill command and we are just about done.

```
colors = [col1, col2];
alphas = [100, 100];
ratios = [0, 255];
matrix = {matrixType:"box", x:0, y:0, h:400, w:550, r:0};
_root.clear();
beginGradientFill("linear", colors, alphas, ratios, matrix);
_root.lineTo(550, 0);
_root.lineTo(550, 400);
_root.lineTo(0, 400);
_root.lineTo(0, 0);
_root.endFill();
```

Now we have some *dynamic* colors in our array, rather than the fixed ones we had before. Note that you can do this with any of the numeric parameters – alpha, ratios, x, y, h, w, r! I'll leave you to investigate all the possibilities. For my final file, I just chose to mess with the rotation factor. I set a rotSpeed variable and a rotAngle and used the sin of that times Math.PI. This left me with a value of −Math.PI to +Math.PI radians of rotation, which is equivalent to -180 to +180 degrees.

Here's the final code, `project_03.fla`. It kind of feels like flying through a rainbow!

```
redSpeed1 = .1;
greenSpeed1 = .07;
blueSpeed1 = .04;
redSpeed2 = .09;
greenSpeed2 = .06;
blueSpeed2 = .03;
rotSpeed = .01;
_root.onEnterFrame = function () {
    redAngle1 += redSpeed1;
    greenAngle1 += greenSpeed1;
    blueAngle1 += blueSpeed1;
    redAngle2 += redSpeed2;
    greenAngle2 += greenSpeed2;
    blueAngle2 += blueSpeed2;
    red1 = Math.sin(redAngle1)*127+128;
    green1 = Math.sin(greenAngle1)*127+128;
    blue1 = Math.sin(blueAngle1)*127+128;
    red2 = Math.sin(redAngle2)*127+128;
    green2 = Math.sin(greenAngle2)*127+128;
    blue2 = Math.sin(blueAngle2)*127+128;
    col1 = red1 << 16 | green1 << 8 | blue1;
    col2 = red2 << 16 | green2 << 8 | blue2;
    rot - Math.sin(rotAngle += rotSpeed)*Math.PI;
    colors = [col1, col2];
    alphas = [100, 100];
    ratios = [0, 255];
    matrix = {matrixType:"box", x:0, y:0, h:400, w:550, r:rot};
    clear();
    beginGradientFill("linear", colors, alphas, ratios, matrix);
    lineTo(550, 0);
    lineTo(550, 400);
    lineTo(0, 400);
    lineTo(0, 0);
    endFill();
};
```

Summary

Well, there, we've covered just about all the new drawing API functions. But as much of a cliché as it sounds, this isn't the end, it's just the beginning. The drawing functions are a way to visualize various mathematical formulas and physics concepts. You can take one example, a sine wave, and go crazy with it. You could literally go through every parameter of every drawing command and figure out how to apply a sine wave to it. We did it for the positions of lines, and the composite colors in a gradient fill. You could try it on the width of lines you are drawing, creating lines that get thin and thick. Or apply it to alpha, having lines or shapes that fade in and out. Or rotation, scale, position, alpha of movie clips that you are drawing into.

When you've completely exhausted `Math.sin`, grab another concept like springs. Don't just spring positions of things – spring their scale or color or rotation! (hmmm...I just gave myself an idea...) Then see how you can combine sine waves with springs.

There are probably about a dozen mathematical formulas and physics principles that I base all my work on. I just think up new ways of combining pieces of this with bits of that and imagine new ways to visualize things. Sometimes I even come up with something that amazes me!

the power of the interval

jared tarbell

essentially, the *Interval* has given us the ability to control time. Quantified time. The ability to control execution based on the passage of time is fundamental to Flash: objects spring to life from their slot on the timeline.

The timeline, however, while being linear and tidy, is not a precise progression of time. The developer specifies each movie's frame rate (measured as frames per second), but that point of reference morphs uncontrollably as it passes through the Flash player. Affected by variable processor demand and speeds, the frame rate can be seriously offset from the specification.

When we are controlling objects and their behavior in digital space, time becomes the only reference point we have to what's really going on. The sleek and efficient use of the Interval delivers us from anomalous imprecision of the frame rate to a more precise system of events and function.

The Interval is a pragmatic concept that enables the developer to define periods of time in which certain functions will be executed.

Why is the Interval so powerful?

The new Interval and its associated functions `setInterval`, `clearInterval`, and `updateAfterEvent` get me most excited about Flash MX. The Interval object provides a framework by which to execute functions at some predefined interval of time, measured in milliseconds. The object is created and destroyed by the two methods `setInterval` and `clearInterval`, respectively. The third method, `updateAfterEvent`, exists to enable the refreshing of the display when Interval events begin to occur faster than the frame rate.

The Interval is precise

The time span between Interval events is measured in milliseconds. Keep in mind that there are one thousand milliseconds in each second. The interval is not as susceptible to frame loss as other movie clip methods. This enables the programmer a high degree of trust when using the Interval. This trust promotes confidence. Confidence makes for better programs. Better programs will save the world from tedium.

The Interval allows faster than normal computation

Previously in Flash, any change made to objects on the stage required that they be rendered before another change could occur. While Flash is exceptionally well adapted for fast rendering (even with anti-aliasing!), this 'render after change' method hindered the programmer from performing complex multi-step interactive computations faster than the frame rate of the movie. The Interval is not bound to the frame rate of the movie. Although not entirely possible on all processors, setting the Interval for a time span of one-millisecond produces an equivalent computational frame rate of about 1000 frames per second.

The Interval can be created and destroyed at will

Not only can the interval be created and destroyed at will but the Interval can also be assigned to multiple objects. Also, multiple Intervals can be assigned to a single object. This has far reaching potential, as we will see in one of our example programs later in the chapter.

he Interval is fast

ide by side comparisons of the Interval and an equivalent frame looping movie clip show
hat the Interval is far less likely to experience latency. Although I don't entirely understand
he object model used to implement the Interval, I can imagine that it's a bit closer to the
netal, and has a much cleaner bit-wise representation during execution.

low do we use the Interval?

Many Flash developers are familiar with the two frame looping movie clip. Typically, the first
rame contains some kind of logical computation to be performed, and the second frame
ontains a single gotoAndPlay(1), sometimes with a terminating conditional. The first
dvantage to the interval is that it can be instantiated anywhere within the timeline, at any
cope, without an object on stage. The interval is set much like an internal register. The inter-
al is now the perfect alternative for anyone who is accustomed to creating small frame
ooping movie clips as logical controllers.

n Flash 5, the standard two frame loop basically went like this:

Frame 1:
```
Some actions to perform...
```

Frame 2:
```
gotoAndPlay(1);
```

Often these objects would exist on the stage to be used as controllers. The same thing can
e accomplished using setInterval with only one line of code and requiring no movie clips
n stage or in the library.

ranscendence from the two frame loop has the advantage of allowing the explicit genera-
ion of computational structures. By replacing the for loop with an Interval,

```
for(i;i<limit;i++) {
    // build some stuff...
}
```

ecomes...

```
function buildSomeStuff(i) {
if (i>=limit) clearInterval(forInterval);
// build some stuff...
}
forInterval = setInterval(stage,"buildSomeStuff",30,i++);
```

We can display the progress of our iterative loop *as it happens*. This is advantageous when
he construction process is interesting, or when the final form has some special meaning
lerived from the process.

Goodbye Loops, hello World

Let's look at an example of the setInterval function in its most basic form:

```
// ActionScript from helloworldtrace.fla, root, Frame 1, Layer logic
 setInterval(function() { trace("hello world"); },1000);
```

From the developer's perspective, the output of the above would look something like this:

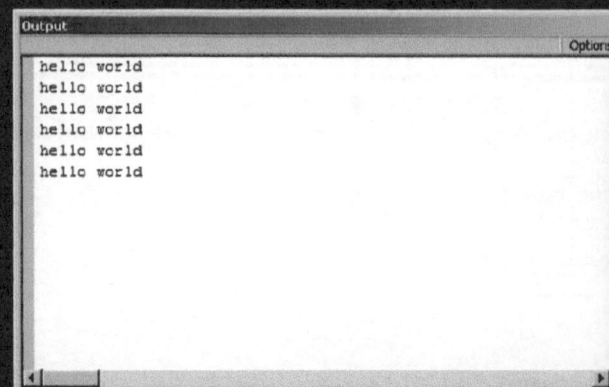

That's not very exciting, so let's do the same thing with a little bit of what Flash excels at, the dynamic creation of vectored text.

Most of the code for the project exists in the first frame of the root timeline:

```
// ActionScript from helloworld.fla, root, Layer logic, Frame 1
function helloWorld() {
    neo="mc"+String(depth++);
    this.attachMovie("mCHello",neo,depth);
    this[neo]._x=_xmouse;
    this[neo]._y=_ymouse;
}
setInterval(this, "helloWorld", 100);
stop();
```

While the function and the setInterval method that references it are both on the same frame and layer, this does not necessarily have to be the case. As long as the function and the setInterval that references it are in the same scope, the process will work.

A movie clip named mcHello exists in the library that is basically a "hello world" text object with a simple expanding shape tween spanning 80 frames. Once instantiated, the movie clip slowly fades forward and decreases in opacity, with a sharp and sudden death as a result of a single line of ActionScript in the very last frame:

```
// ActionScript from helloworld.fla, Movieclip mcHello, Layer logic,
 Frame 1
 this.removeMovieClip();
```

The final effect of this movie is a one second clock that beats out a smoothly animated 'hello World' from the user's mouse position.

Virtually everything in the rest of this chapter is based on this simple idea. Pretty neat. Let's look at how the Interval is implemented in ActionScript.

setInterval

The `setInterval` method encapsulates the core functionality of the new Interval and is the most commonly used of all three Interval methods. In short, the `setInterval` function defines a specific function to be called as some specified time interval, as applied to a specific object within the movie.

clearInterval

The `clearInterval` method is used to clear an Interval set by `setInterval`. If we plan on removing an Interval at some point in the future, we need to keep track of it. This is accomplished by grabbing the name of the Interval through the return object of the function. When calling `clearInterval`, we simply pass to it the name of the Interval we wish to be destroyed.

```
myInterval = setInterval( function () { trace("ping") },1000);
```

Later we rid ourselves with...

```
clearInterval(myInterval);
```

updateAfterEvent

An interesting feature of the `setInterval` function is the ability to create Intervals that are faster than the frame rate of the movie clip. This has some peculiar consequences because the Flash player only draws the screen after the calculation of each frame. When computations begin to occur multiple times within the same frame, some computations are not rendered to the screen.

The `updateAfterEvent` function exists to force the Flash Player to redraw the screen, regardless of frame rate. The method is processor intensive, and essentially involves a temporary increase in frame rate to compensate for Intervals faster than the frame rate or in between frames.

A particularly useful thing to know about Flash MX is that it will halt frame execution to completely process all script within a particular frame. The positive aspect of this behavior is that we are assured all code will be executed. The negative effect of this behavior is that in cases where the code's execution time is great, animation frames can be lost, resulting in a lower frame rate. This is often referred to as frame loss. The Interval helps us avoid this pitfall by not requiring the Flash player to redraw the screen after every step. In cases where it is important to see each step of interface generation, the `updateAfterEvent` function will force the display to redraw regardless of the current position of the playhead.

Use the `updateAfterEvent` method if it's important that a computational update be immediately represented on the display.

Variations of use

Macromedia has allowed us a couple of different ways to assign Intervals to objects other than object indifferent assignment in the root timeline. We'll go through each of these methods by applying them to the specific instances where they are most useful. In each case the FLAs I've made are available for download from www.friendsofED.com, and as we're investigating the new features of MX here you may like to investigate these to further understand how the effects are created – looking at other people's work is a great way to learn. Before every piece of script in the chapter I've added a comment showing exactly where in the FLA it can be found.

Building a clock with parameterized intervals

I have often found myself obsessing over the construction of a time display with each new programming language I begin working in. Flash is no exception, nor am I the only one who does this. The clock is sometimes an unnecessarily heavy gravitation in a programmer's life. Quite simply, building clock faces is an interesting recreation.

Let's use the new found simplicity of `setInterval` to build ourselves a parameterized clock. By allowing our clock to work off a set of custom definable parameters, we unhinge ourselves from the standard system clock. This detachment from 'real time' will provide a nice space to get more creative.

The approach in previous versions would be to periodically read values from the Date object and interpret them in some graphical way. Values would be stored as commonly held units of time in the form of seconds, minutes, hours, and sometimes a specific day in the human continuum. The `setInterval` defines frequency of execution using milliseconds, still a common time unit, but small enough as to be practically indistinguishable to most humans. Remember that there are 1000 milliseconds in one second. I might take a guess and estimate that over 500,000 milliseconds have flown by since you began reading this chapter.

Our movie is exactly one frame, it is `stack.fla` - available for download at www.friendsofED.com. At the root level of our movie, frame 1 has this script:

```
// ActionScript stack.fla, root, Layer logic, Frame 1
// basic unit of time
scalar=30;
// clock stack intervals
picoInterval = setInterval(function () {
colorColA.gotoAndStop(colorColA._currentframe+1);},scalar);
nanoInterval = setInterval(function () {
colorColB.gotoAndStop(colorColB._currentframe+1);
colorColA.gotoAndStop(1); },scalar*50);
decoInterval = setInterval(function () {
colorColC.gotoAndStop(colorColC._currentframe+1);
colorColB.gotoAndStop(1); },scalar*500);
stop();
```

Note the use of a multiplier in the form of a variable called `scalar`. Setting up the relationships between clock units in this fashion allows us a quick and easy way to adjust the timing of all three intervals with a single variable.

Our clock will work on a basic premise. We have three movie clips at the `_root` level. Each of the movie clips contains a number of frames, each frame with a stack of colored bars one greater than the frame before. Playing one of these movie clips straight through would show what would appear to be colored bars, stacking up on top of each other.

Using Intervals, we will control the rate by which each of these three movie clips plays itself. Each passing of time will advance the playhead for the corresponding movie clip by exactly one. Movie clips that represent higher orders of time (units of time that contain other units of time) also reset the playheads of those units back to frame 1. The end result is a stacking clock that works independent of the system `Date` object and on arbitrarily defined units of time.

Each movie clip contains only one bit of logic on the first frame:

```
stop();
```

Really, that's all we need to do. We are free to use the rest of the `_root`'s timeline for whatever purposes we wish. The clock will run until the movie is closed because that is the nature and fundamental power of the Interval.

Running our clock produces a beautiful cascading representation of time slipping by. Watching the clock for only a few seconds shows us the patterns by which it is operating.

To produce astounding effects, we might make quick modifications to the graphic content stored on each frame of the three clock unit movie clips. Even simpler, we could replace the movie clips with something new altogether. Try placing a short animation you may have from another project into the Library. Drag three instances of the animation onto the main stage, and name them `ColorColA`, `ColorColB`, and `ColorColC`, respectively. The resulting clock will be an abstract collage of animation across multiple frames of time.

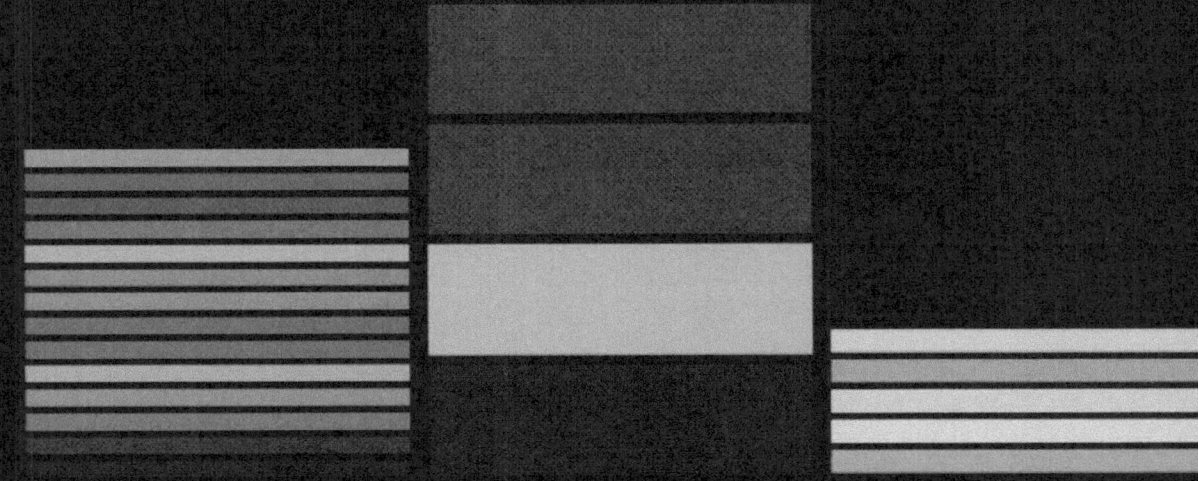

Generative computations using the Interval

If I could cast a magic spell, my first spell would be the creation of an eternal vine, thick with strength, green and soft. A vine big enough to climb, right up into the clouds to an unknown world of swirling water vapor, tiny bacterium, and thunderous electrical activity. I suppose I would probably want to dress up a bit, and pack some food. Or could I conjure up that as well?

It's a ridiculous question. Casting magic spells is simply not possible. Perhaps that's why we program. The majesty and wonder of programming is conjuring the ethereal out of nowhere, and forming it into your heart's desire. Even better, these apparitions of light, magic, and code are reactive! They live, and as they do, they make decisions, they respond to interaction, they learn, they accumulate, they combine, and they die. No need to get too attached to these guys, for perhaps the most wonderful thing about them is that their reality is defined as a repeatable statement, spread across wire and replicated on storage devices around the globe. Killing one of them off is not necessarily the end of their existence as a species. We'll just instantiate another one or maybe another few thousand.

A dilemma of generative design is showing the construction process of a computationally generated structure as it happens. Normally, the programmer has a few choices that are basically grouped in one of two ways: those processes that show the construction of the computations as they happen, and those processes that show the generated structure after all computations have been done. From the user's perspective, the former is often more exciting (unless the process takes too long). Of course it is also often more difficult to program. This is especially true in older versions of Flash, where both computation and display were frame-based processes. Flash MX is still primarily the same, however the Interval allows us to circumnavigate this restriction.

Let's get to work on our first incantation!

Time-based texturing

Here's a fun example that provides the user direct control over two unique generative Intervals through the press of a button. For demonstration purposes, I've written each function using two alternate methods of setInterval.

The movie is simple: two frames, two layers (called logic and button). On the layer called button, frame 1, we have a button that sends the playhead to frame 4. On layer button, frame 4, we have a button that sends the playhead to frame 1.

On the layer named logic, frame 1, we have the following code:

```
// ActionScript from texture.fla, root, Frame 1, Layer logic
clearInterval(intvTwo);
intvOne = setInterval(function() {
    neo="dot"+String(_root.depth++);
    _root.createEmptyMovieClip(neo, _root.depth);
    with (_root[neo]) {
        lineStyle(1,0x746963,30);
        curveTo(10,10+random(30),500,0);
```

```
        _x=random(500);
        _y=random(500);
    }
},10);
stop();
```

On layer logic, frame 4, we have the following code:

```
// ActionScript from texture.fla, root, Layer logic, Frame 4
clearInterval(intvOne);
function makeNeo() {
    neo="dot"+String(depth++);
    this.createEmptyMovieClip(neo, depth);
    with (this[neo]) {
      lineStyle(1,0x736975,30);
      curveTo(-10,10+random(30),-500,0);
      _x=random(500);
      _y=random(500);
    }
}
intvTwo = setInterval(this,"makeNeo",10);
stop();
```

The logic performed on both frames is equivalent. Frame 1 uses a style in which the function definition is embedded as a parameter to the setInterval method. It draws brown lines. Frame 4 uses a style in which a function is defined externally, and referenced by name as a parameter of the setInterval. It draws blue lines. Both styles work equally well. Both have their own advantages.

Notice that both styles clear the Interval of the other as a first step. Failing to do this would result in a 'doubling' generative effect each time the user pressed the button. It would also creep dangerously towards the heart of the CPU like a tiger in the brush.

The result of this movie is a system in which nicely colored curves slowly populate the display area, producing a polychromatic feathered texture. Since we're giving the user some degree of control (they decide which Interval is executed and for how long), the results of the system are unique and boundless.

Let's get to work on a level two incantation: the beanstalk!

Recursive beanstalk and the 'one time' Interval

The recursively-generated object is now a familiar form. It would be interesting to watch such a form take shape under the constraints of a series of time Intervals. We might grow a vine or stalk that would ebb and flow to an unseen season. That would be nice.

Let's attempt to do this, the FLA we're about to create is available for download as beanstalk.fla. First, for reasons we will discuss later, we will set an Interval on the root level that periodically calculates a sine curve based on a randomly increasing value. Then we stop. The code on frame 1 looks like this:

```
// ActionScript beanstalk.fla, root, Layer logic, Frame 1
// curly effect
sinusoidal = new Object();
sinusoidal.wobble = function() {
      _root.t+=random(41)/2;
      _root.sint=30*Math.sin(Math.PI / 180 * _root.t);
      }
setInterval(sinusoidal,"wobble",60);
stop();
```

This simply sets up an oscillating vector at the root level that can be referenced by instantiated movie clips to determine their rotation. The end effect of such a system is an irregular curling effect. We will need no additional code on the root level.

Let's now create the basic building block of our beanstalk, the 'node' movie clip. Two instances of this movie clip sit in the center of the stage in the root timeline. They are the basic building blocks of our magic vine.

Create a new movie clip, called 'node', and link it for ActionScript export with the same name. Draw a basic geometric shape on stage and center it to the origin of the movie clip. This shape, whatever it may be, will be the repeated shape that eventually builds our beanstalk.

Now create a new layer called logic and place the following ActionScript on the first frame:

```
// ActionScript beanstalk.fla, node Movieclip, Layer logic, Frame 1
// do not grow beyond 100 nested nodes
if (depth<100) {
    growInterval=setInterval(this,"grow",30);
    // at random, generate an offshoot
    if (!random(depth+5)) sproutNewGrowth();
}
stop();
```

Notice that we are essentially doing three things: checking the depth to see if we are not too deep to continue, setting up an Interval to call the function 'grow' every 30 milliseconds, and we're creating a quick random test to occasionally create new sprout growth.

We also need to write the two functions that are referenced by the above. For consistency, let's create a new layer called functions and put them there. They look like this:

```
// ActionScript beanstalk.fla, node Movieclip, Layer functions, Frame 1

// function grow
// Adds a new node of recursive growth to the vine
function grow() {
    // attach a new Movieclip called 'nd'
    neo="nd";
    this.attachMovie("node",neo,0);
    this[neo]._y=-100;
    // reference the sinusoidal on the root level to twist gracefully
    this[neo]._rotation=_root.sint;
    // slight reduction in size
    this[neo]._xscale=99;
    this[neo]._yscale=99;
    this[neo].depth=this.depth+1;
    // no need to grow more than once
    // clear the growing interval
    clearInterval(this.growInterval);
}

// function sproutNewGrowth
// Creates a small branch of growth (sprouts)
function sproutNewGrowth() {
    // attach a new Movieclip, uniquely named 'limb1', 'limb2', 'limb3'…
    neo="limb"+String(_root.depth++);
    _root.attachMovie("node",neo,_root.depth);

    // determine the root level position to put the growth
    var point = new object();
    point.x = 0;
    point.y = 0;
    localToGlobal(point);
    _root[neo]._x=point.x;
    _root[neo]._y=point.y;

    // half growth to the left, half grow to the right
    if (random(2)) {
      _root[neo]._rotation=_root.sint+90;
    } else {
      _root[neo]._rotation=_root.sint-90;
    }

    // make the new sprout very small
    _root[neo]._xscale=5;
    _root[neo]._yscale=5;
```

```
    _root[neo].depth=depth;
  }
```

Both of these functions are standard recursive processes that attach the same movie clip within itself, over and over again, each time with some small twist (determined by the vector at the root level) and a slight reduction in size. Notice however, the `clearInterval` function at the very end of the `grow` function. This `clearInterval` function clears the very Interval that called the function in the first place. Why would we want to do this? Well, quite simply, we only want the function to be called once. In this case, we are leveraging the Interval as a delay.

What would happen if we didn't clear the Interval? Due to the recursive nature of this function, we would end up establishing Intervals exponentially, quickly consuming all available resources on the host machine, most probably bringing the operating system to its knees.

Using this simple structure as a basis of experimentation, we can climb great distances into far away clouds. Before I could help myself, I was already changing the color of the 'node' movie clip and even added a second frame to it that contained a flower. Since flowers are not as common as the node structures upon which they grow, I only allow the 'node' movie clip to stop on this frame every 42 or so instantiations (approximately 2% of all nodes will also have a flower). To accomplish this, we need only one additional line of code in the first frame of the 'node' movie clip:

```
// ActionScript beanstalk2.fla, node Movieclip, Layer functions, Frame 1
if (random(42)) stop();
```

Of course we would also need to place a `stop()` on frame 2 so that we don't loop back to the beginning. This particular version of the beanstalk is available for download as `beanstalk2.fla`.

It's always nice to be able to create an object in Flash and then forget about it. Objects that allow this usually have some degree of logical intelligence, or in sharp contrast, are quite boring, just sitting around on the stage often exactly where you left them. For this next example, I would like to demonstrate how we might create a small universe of the former type of object using the `setInterval` as the mechanism of intelligence.

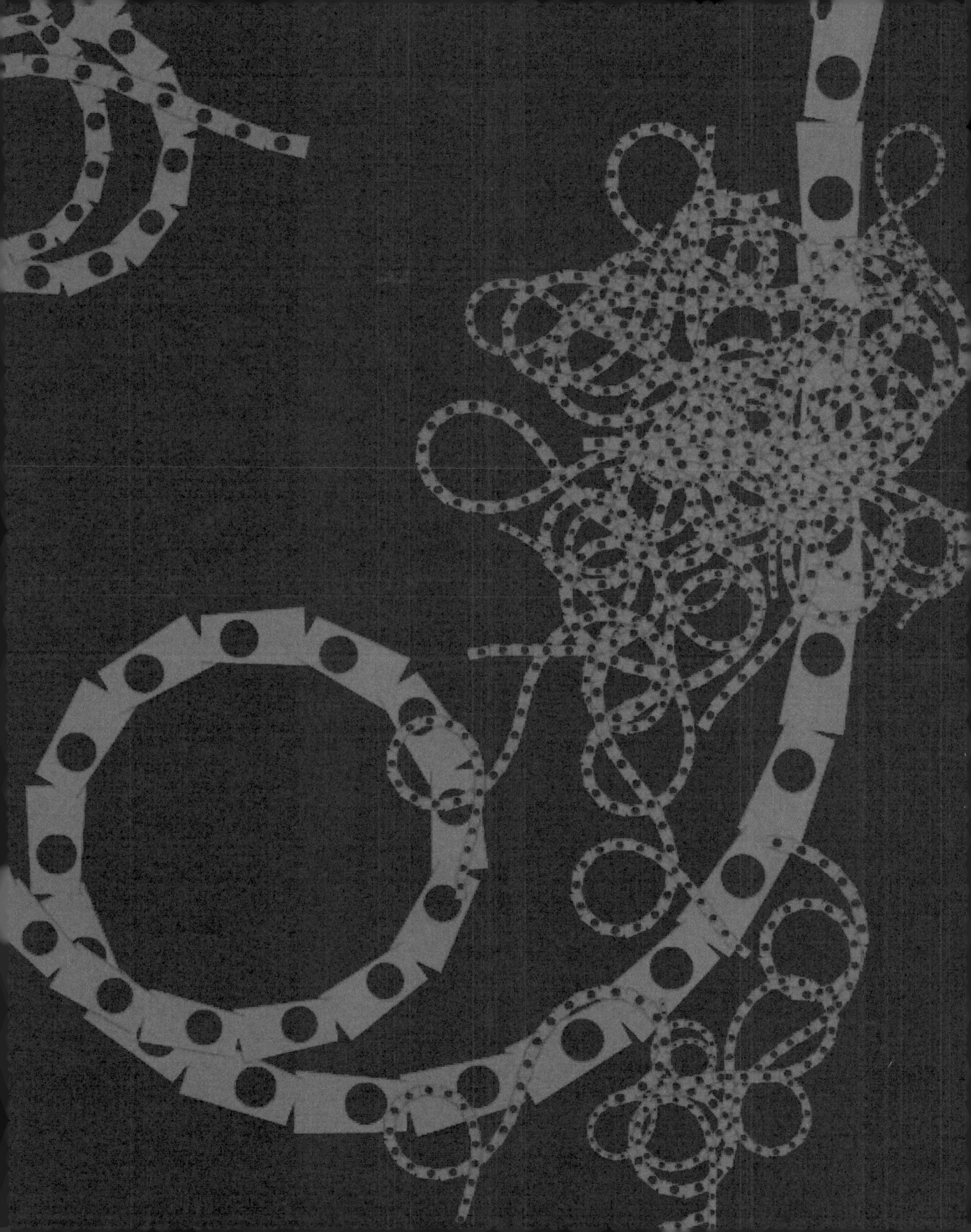

Flyers

Create a new movie clip. Call it 'ringSource' and place exactly one copy onto the stage. Export the movie clip for ActionScript using the same name for its link identifier. Inside the movie clip, rename the single layer 'logic' and apply the following ActionScript to frame 1:

```
// ActionScript from flyers.fla, ringSource Movieclip, Frame 1, Layer logic
function produceFlyer() {
    neo="fly"+String(depth++);
    this.attachMovie("flyer",neo,depth);
    rot=random(360);
    this[neo]._rotation=rot;
    this[neo].vy=6*Math.sin(Math.PI/180*rot);
    this[neo].vx=6*Math.cos(Math.PI/180*rot);
}
rotInterval = setInterval(function () { _rotation-=1 },30);
proInterval = setInterval(this,"produceFlyer",100);
stop();
```

By this code segment, we can see that there are two functions to assign to the ringSource. One function simply rotates it by one degree every 30 milliseconds and the other is used to produce something called a flyer that we will soon discuss.

The flyer is a movie clip that we will need to create; it's a small graphic object that follows the 'create and abandon' methodology we discussed earlier. It contains two functions, die and move. These functions do basically what they describe. The functions are executed as part of an Interval, however, only one function is executed at a time. This is because we want the 'flyer' to move about and live for a while before we send him off into a confused death spiral, where ultimately, we force him to remove himself.

```
// ActionScript from flyers.fla, flyer Movieclip, Frame 1, Layer logic
function die() {
    this._y+=vy;
    this._x+=vx;
    this._xscale+=vs;
    this._yscale+=vs;
    vx+=(random(7)-3)/10;
    vy+=(random(7)-3)/10;
    vs+=(random(7)-3)/5;
    this._alpha-=1;
    age++;
    if (age>300) {
        clearInterval(dieInterval);
        this.removeMovieClip();
    }
}
function move() {
    this._y+=vy;
    this._x+=vx;
    this._xscale+=vs;
    this._yscale+=vs;
```

```
    vs+=(random(7)-3)/5;
    vx*=.97;
    vy*=.97;
    age++;
    if (age>200) {
      clearInterval(moveInterval);
      dieInterval = setInterval(this,"die",20);
    }
  }
  moveInterval = setInterval(this,"move",20);
  stop();
```

Notice how behavioral control of the movie clip is self-governing. Initially, the 'flyer' sets up a single Interval to be executed at the relatively short time space of 20 milliseconds. Within the function called by the Interval (namely move), an age variable is increment each time through. Once the 'flyer' reaches a certain age (201), the original Interval is cleared and a new one is set up, this time referencing the die function.

This same functionality could be accomplished using clip events, in particular, enterFrame. However, clip events apply only to movie clips already placed on stage, and thus do not persist when a movie clip is attached from the Library.

The die function does a number of things similar to the move function. Position is adjusted, velocities are modified, and age is incremented. The fundamental difference is that the die function introduces a heaping portion of chaos through randomization. There is also a more severe age conditional: when the age reaches a certain limit (300), the final Interval is cleared and the movie clip removes itself from existence. This is what is meant by create and abandon, as no computational work outside the movie clip is required once it has been instantiated.

A variation on this theme introduces an alternative graphic shape and new functionality.

Instead of each instantiated movie clip existing as a lonely nomad, oblivious to the entities around him, we'll allow each flyer movie clip to have precisely one friend. The friend will simply be the flyer previously created. Later, we'll write a function that shows these friendly relationships, but first, we must tell each newly created flyer exactly who his friend is. I'll use the variable friend, because that seems appropriate. Friend will store the name of the other flyer movie clip. The following code exists in the function produceFlyer() of the ringSource movie clip:

```
// ActionScript from flyers.fla, ringSource Movieclip, Frame 1, Layer logic
  this[neo].friend="flyguy"+String(depth-2);
```

There are now many things a flyer can accomplish knowing the name of another flyer. For this example, we'll simply have each flyer draw a line to his friend. This is not just a normal line however. Our flyers are moving all over the place, so drawing a line must be a dynamic process. Again, an Interval will accomplish this task with ease:

```
// ActionScript from flyers.fla, flyer Movieclip, Frame 1, Layer logic
  function lineToFriend() {
      this.clear();
      this.lineStyle(0,0xffffff,20);
      this.lineTo(_parent[this.friend]._x-this._x,_parent[this.friend]._y-this._y);
  }
  lineInterval =setInterval(this,"lineToFriend",30);
```

The result is an intricate relational system of friendly flyers.

Simulating: a randomly connected binary switch network

Precision is an important part of simulation. In an object oriented environment, we must be mindful of concurrence. To demonstrate how we might use the Interval as the driver behind a successful simulation, let's build a network of interconnected switches, which if created successfully, will have some very unusual properties.

The premise for our network of movie clips is fairly straightforward. Each movie clip is a switch that can be either 'on' or 'off'. Switches are randomly connected to other switches. The state of the switch is determined by the state of the switches to which it is connected through some simple set of rules. For our example, let's use the following two rules (changing these rules would be a fruitful path of creative exploration):

Switching rules
Each switch is connected to at least two other switches.
A switch moves into the 'on' state if exactly one of the connected switches is also 'on'.

As a first step, let's create the binary switch.

Create a new movie clip and name it 'node'. Rename the first layer 'logic', and add another layer called 'graphic'. This way we can easily separate code from the graphic shapes, something we may be changing frequently until we get the look we desire.

Basically, the switch will be a three-frame movie clip. The first frame contains the logic we will use to set up the node's Interval and the other two frames are used to maintain node state:

```
// ActionScript from network.fla, node, Layer logic, Frame 1
connectList = new Array();
var nextState;
if (random(2)) gotoAndPlay("off");
```

Frames two and three in the Logic layer are labeled "on" and "off", respectively. By default, the switch will initially be set to some random state (see the script in frame 1). A unique graphic shape illustrates the node's state and sits on the stage of each frame. The appearance of the switch is entirely up to you. For this example, I've used a solid white square for the "on" state and a gray square outline for the "off" state. The idea here is that the "on" state is somehow lit up.

Each node has three functions. They are called by network control logic found in the root timeline, the details of which will be discussed later. The functions must be accessible to each state of the node, so rather than redefine each function on those frames in the Logic layer, let's create a new layer called Functions that spans all frames of the movie clip and contains the following ActionScript:

```
// ActionScript from network.fla, node, Frame 1, Layer functions
function connectTo(esta) {
    lineStyle(0,0xffffff,20);
    moveTo(0,0);
    lineTo(_root[esta]._x-this._x, _root[esta]._y-this._y);
    connectList.push(esta);
}
function calcNext() {
    var charge=0;
    for (n=0;n<connectList.length;n++) {
        if (_root[connectList[n]].state=="on") charge++;
```

```
    }
    if (charge%2) nextState="on";
    else nextState="off";
}
function setNext() {
    this.gotoAndPlay(nextState);
}
```

As a final step, export the switch movie clip for ActionScript using the link identifier 'node'. We now have a fully configured binary switch, ready to be assembled into a network.

Our movie then, really consists of three stages: build the network, randomly connect the switches and as a final step, watch the simulation unfold.

We have a couple of thousand choices on how we might arrange nodes within our network. Fortunately, the physical laws of microelectronic circuitry do not bind us. To keep things simple, I have decided to arrange our network in a simple grid of equal length and width. The algorithm to build such a network is as follows:

```
// ActionScript from network.fla, root, Layer logic, Frame 1
network = new Array();
// make network
for (x=0; x<4; x++) {
    for (y=0; y<4; y++) {
        neo = "node"+String(depth++);
        this.attachMovie("node", neo, depth);
        this[neo]._x = 120+x*40;
        this[neo]._y = 120+y*40;
        // register the name of the switch by placing it in an array
        network.push(neo);
    }
}
```

Notice we used two simple for loops. We could have done the same thing with an Interval, but for this specific purpose (arranging items in a grid) the loop is absolutely perfect. Besides, soon enough we'll have plenty of Intervals running.

Next, we need to connect our nodes to each other in a sufficiently random fashion. For this, we will use another for loop in the next frame. It is not critical that we avoid overloading connections (connecting to the same switch twice), nor is it one of our rules. However, as a logical precaution we will avoid connecting switches to themselves. As such, the following will work just fine:

```
// ActionScript from network.fla, root, Layer logic, Frame 2
for (m=0;m<2;m++) {
    for (n=0;n<network.length;n++) {
        neo=network[n];
        esta=n;
        while (esta==n) {
            esta=random(network.length);
        }
        this[neo].connectTo(network[esta]);
    }
}
```

Next, we need to set our simulation in motion. The switching logic for our network will be controlled from the root timeline using a single Interval:

```
// ActionScript from network.fla, root, Layer logic, Frame 2
cycle = new Object();
cycle.interval = function() {
    var n;
    // compute next state for all switches
    for (n=0; n<network.length; n++) {
        _root[network[n]].calcNext();
    }
    // change state of all switches
    for (n=0; n<network.length; n++) {
        _root[network[n]].setNext();
    }
}
cycleInterval = setInterval(cycle, "interval", 100);
stop();
```

Although not exactly simple, that's it! We've now defined a system often referred to as a randomly connected binary network.

Generate a few random networks and observe the switching behavior of the nodes as a collective. Do you see isolated areas of pattern? Do you see randomness? Do you see waves of repeated switching sequences traveling the network? Stare long enough, and you will observe all of these phenomena.

The most interesting aspect of building any system is discovering properties of that system that one wouldn't normally expect. Such is the case with the randomly connected binary network. In addition to producing surprising behavior, the binary network is a useful tool for emulating computational neurosciences, including memory and analytical thinking.

Building networks with sufficiently large numbers of switches promotes environments of adaptation and thought process. The question then becomes one of magnitude. What is the threshold of complexity required for an adaptive, thinking system? Certainly it is well above the 49 or so switching elements we are using in our Flash example. Still, there are some interesting effects that can be observed through watching these small-scale binary networks.

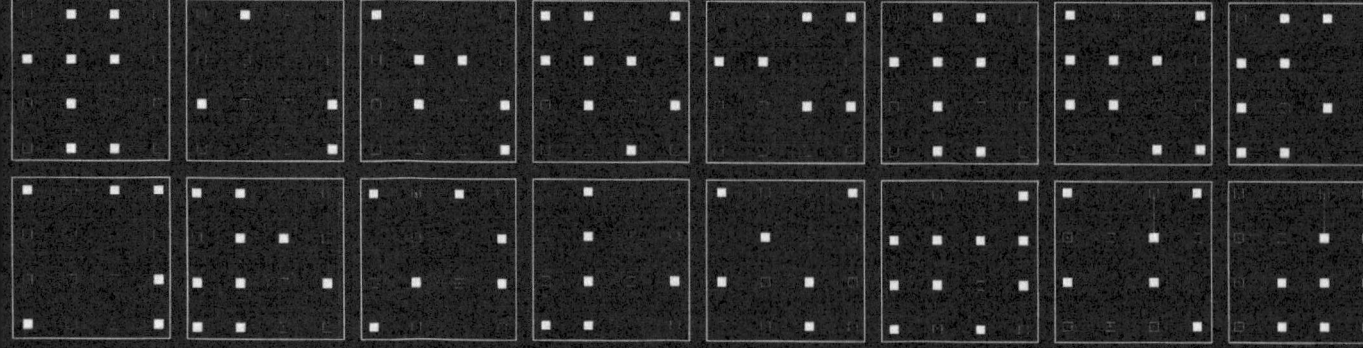

Particles exhibiting variable blur

Let's look at an example that uses the Interval to govern the extent by which user control is monitored. This is a useful method for conserving CPU usage when precision user control is not necessarily required or when user control has profound effects on computational requirements. A high animation frame rate can be maintained while the user's input is only periodically collected at a substantially slower rate.

In this example, small spherical objects wander mindlessly in three-dimensional space. Using the position of the mouse, interaction with the objects adjusts the hysteria and speed by which they wander. This is done with clever use of the Interval and is a good example of what could not be done in Flash 5 before this version. In previous versions of Flash, we would have run into a brick wall trying to force these objects faster than the frame rate.

First, create a layer named logic and assign the following ActionScript to it:

```
// ActionScript from blurbits.fla, _root, Frame 1, Layer logic

// set up mousewatch
mouseWatch = new Object();
mouseWatch.interval = function() {
  // watch the mouse and do stuff
  bitChange=Math.ceil(60*Math.abs(_xmouse/600));
  bitSpeed=Math.ceil(30*Math.abs(_ymouse/350));
  for (n=0;n<_root.bitList.length;n++) {
    _root[_root.bitList[n]].updateInterval(_root.bitSpeed);
  }
}

// set the user input interval around 10 fps
mouseInterval = setInterval( mouseWatch, "interval", 100);
```

The above has accomplished a few important things for us. First, we've created an object called mouseWatch and defined a single function for it, called interval. Using the current position of the mouse, this function sets two important root level variables called bitChange and bitSpeed. They are measurements in milliseconds that all moving objects on stage reference to determine behavior.

bitChange controls how often the moving objects on stage will arbitrarily choose a new destination. bitSpeed determines how fast the objects move.

There's a bit of mathematics used to adjust the value ranges of both bitChange and bitSpeed to acceptable levels.

bitChange is computed starting from the inside out. First, we unitize the horizontal position of the mouse into a range of [0...1]. This is assuming that the width of the stage is exactly 600 pixels. What we can't assume is that the mouse will stay within the stage. It may move to the left of zero, and this would give us a negative value. We do not want negative values! To avoid this we take the absolute value. Multiplying this by a constant of 60 should then return a number between 0 and 60 (maybe higher). As a final step, we take the ceiling value, which rounds the number up to the nearest whole number. In our case, this value represents the nearest millisecond.

BitSpeed is computed similarly, the only differences lying in the constants and the cardinality of the mouse.

Basically, the closer the mouse is to the top left corner, the faster and more wild the bits on the screen are going to fly around. As a final step, the function iterates through the list of existing bits and adjusts their intervals to reflect the new values of the bit variables.
The root timeline also contains two additional lines of code:

```
// ActionScript from blurbits.fla, _root, Frame 1, Layer logic

// registry of all bits
bitList = new Array();

// some bits on the screen incantation (x origin, y origin, number of bits)
genRandomBits(300,175,10);
```

The first sets up an array for bits to register themselves when they are created. The second generates a few random bits to get things started.

Create another layer named functions. Here we will keep the genRandomBits function, used to create some iBits.

```
// ActionScript from blurbits.fla, _root, Frame // 1, Layer functions
function genRandomBits(x,y,num) {
    // create a number of bits at a position: x,y
    for (n=0;n<num;n++) {
      neo="bit"+String(depth++);
      this.attachMovie("ibit",neo,10+depth);
      this[neo]._x=x;
      this[neo]._y=y;
      // register the name of this new iBit
      this.bitList.push(neo);
    }
}
```

Now let's create the movie clip that we will be instantiating. Draw a circle on the root stage and convert it into a movie clip. Call the new movie clip 'iBit' and link it with the same name so that it can be exported for ActionScript. Now edit the movie clip by double-clicking it.

On the first frame, create a layer called logic and apply the following ActionScript to it:

```
// ActionScript from blurbits.fla, iBit
// Movieclip, Frame 1, Layer logic
// set initial destination
dx=random(600);
dy=random(350);
dz=random(100);
// set up interval
intervalMove = setInterval( this, "wander", 30);

stop();
```

Now apply the following ActionScript to the functions layer:

```
// ActionScript from blurbits.fla, iBit Movieclip, Frame 1, Layer functions
function pickDestination() {
    // pick some nearby place to go
    dx+=random(201)-100;
    dy+=random(201)-100;
    dz+=random(50)-25;
    // make sure this hasn't picked some place offstage
    if (dx<0) dx=0;
    else if (dx>600) dx=600;
    if (dy<0) dy=0;
    else if (dy>350) dy=350;
    if (dz<0) dz=0;
    else if (dz>80) dz=80;
}
function updateInterval(newSpeed) {
    // set up intervals - test
    clearInterval(intervalMove);
    intervalMove = setInterval( this, "wander", newSpeed);
}
function wander() {
    // randomly pick new destination
    if (!random(_parent.bitChange)) pickDestination();
    // move to destination
    vx+=(_x-dx)/30;
    vy+=(_y-dy)/30;
    vz+=(z-dz)/30;
    _x-=vx;
    _y-=vy;
    z-=vz;
    _xscale=_yscale=100-z;
    this.blur0._x=vx*.9;
    this.blur0._y=vy*.9;
    this.blur1._x=vx*.6;
    this.blur1._y=vy*.6;
    this.blur2._x=vx*.3;
    this.blur2._y=vy*.3;
    vx*=.8;
    vy*=.8;
    vz*=.8;
}
```

All three functions are critical to the correct behavior of the movie clip, although their specific implementations can be modified to create any number of unusual effects. The `wander` function is used to move the object to its destination in an elegant fashion using an elastic vector and some friction. This is also where the blur circles are offset according to velocity. The `pickDestination` function does exactly what it sounds like it does. These two functions are fairly standard ways to move an object about the screen. It is the `updateInterval` function that is of particular interest to us within the context of this chapter, as that is where the movie clip's movement Interval is adjusted. If you recall, a mouse-watching function in the root timeline makes iterative calls to the `updateInterval` function for each iBit. The function clears the old Interval, then sets a new one with the parameter passed in as an argument. Notice how we've assigned a name to this `setInterval`. This is critical if we are to later remove it.

To reinforce the illusion of fast movement, several layers of additional circles have been placed on lower layers. By offsetting their position relative to the velocity of the object, a blurring effect is created that is quite believable.

The only additional element of the movie is an optional large button that sits in the background. Each time the button is pressed, additional iBits are created through the `genRandomBits` function.

Remove the first the iBit we created on the main stage, and we're ready to set this movie in action.

So what does this 'iBit' behavior look like, exactly? Well, it's basically small spherical object that seems to fly around the screen in three dimensions. The regularity and speed with which s does this is controlled by the position of the mouse, in real time. What's most amazing is when the speed of the bit moves beyond what one would normally consider to be the highest speed possible, given the frame rate. This is nice. Of course this is only possible using the Interval.

Experimental uses and the danger of recursion

Recursion is a particularly dangerous but potentially exciting use of the Interval. Recursion is simply a process where a function is allowed to call itself. Recursion can also be a collection of functions that through their inter-linking, form a kind of feedback loop. Because the `setInterval` calls a function as part of it's execution, creating a recursive structure would simply involve the embedding of another `setInterval` somewhere within the invoking function.

Why is this dangerous?

Recursion is a dangerous proposition because if left unchecked, the process quickly consumes all available resources on a machine and renders its host program emaciated, confused, and useless. This is particularly evident with the use of `setInterval`. `SetInterval` does not make a single call to some function, but rather, makes repeated calls to a function at potentially rapid rates, an infinite number of times, or until it is cleared. It's not hard to understand the severity of what would happen if we started calling Intervals within Intervals.

Let's abandon caution and get right into it!

Even with careful consideration, we have a considerably high chance of locking our machine during these experiments. For this reason, save often! Do not keep open, unsaved work in other applications. Do not expect to halt ActionScript execution by answering 'Yes' if we should hit an infinitely dense computation rate. We may not see that dialog.

Perhaps we should start safely and work our way towards tighter, more elegant algorithms. In this light, here is a recursively defined Interval definition that uses only trace statements to represent its progress:

```
setInterval(function() { trace("army of Intervals");
setInterval(function() { trace("shot fired") },900) }, 1000);
```

The output of the above is a series of messages sent to the Output window. It goes something like:

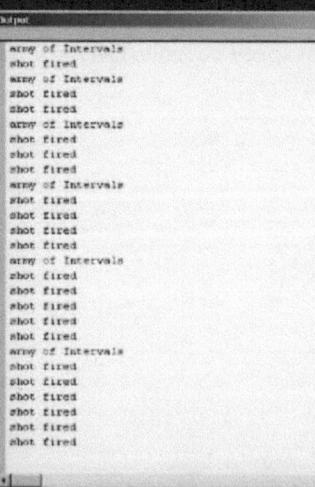

Let's build an example that does the same thing, but with movie clips.

Create a new movie. Rename the main layer to `logic`. Place the following code on the first frame:

```
function stackBrick(bcolor) {
    neo="brick"+String(depth++);
    this.createEmptyMovieClip(neo,depth);
    this[neo]._x=stackWidth;
    this[neo]._y=stackHeight;
    if (bcolor=="blue") {
        this[neo].lineStyle(0,0x94abda,100);
        this[neo].beginFill(0x94abda,100);
    } else {
        this[neo].lineStyle(0,0x454545,100);
        this[neo].beginFill(0x454545,100);
    }
    this[neo].lineTo(0,8);
    this[neo].lineTo(8,8);
    this[neo].lineTo(8,0);
    this[neo].lineTo(0,0);
    stackHeight+=10;
    if (stackHeight>500) {
        stackHeight=0;
        stackWidth+=10;
    }
}
mainInterval = setInterval( function() {
        stackBrick("blue");
            setInterval(function() { stackBrick("brown") },90);
        },100);
stop();
```

Basically, we're setting up the same recursive interval definition as in the previous example. Instead of calling the trace function, we're calling a function of our own, called `stackBrick`.

`stackBrick` is a fairly straightforward MX specific function that leverages the new drawing API. This example simply draws a square, and colors it a specific color based on the function parameter `bcolor`. To stack the bricks properly (not that we necessarily need to avoid unconventional methods), we track the stack's height and width using to incrementally determined variables, `stackHeight` and `stackWidth`, respectively.

That's it! But believe me, this is plenty enough to get us into some serious trouble. Save your work. Some machines may be able to render the background image on this page.

During the execution of this movie, small colored squares stack themselves both vertically and horizontally, filling the screen. The color of each square is determined by the Interval that called it. In this example, we have two Intervals, one associated with blue and the other with gray.

By instantiating a movie clip each time an Interval is called, we can observe the frequency and patterns of their periodicity. The pattern of this example is not as simple as it first appears. For each blue movie clip created, an additional brown movie clip is scheduled to be created. The effect is a cascading series of gray movie clips.

Adjusting the time of the Intervals can produce interesting variations of effect. The time difference between the two Intervals is the important part of the adjustment, not necessary the magnitudes of the time. Adjusting the magnitudes only speeds up or slows down the construction of the pattern.

For this example, I have discovered that I most like Intervals that are very close in their periods of execution. Self-similarity produces subtle variations of pattern. I am hesitant to encourage the experimentation of recursive Interval definition. If you do decide to explore, be sure to save your work often. Avoid malicious publishing, and start off with large time intervals.

scriptable masks

lifaros

I always start by drawing my experiments on a piece of paper, just like a storyboard. Then I try to define the functions that I need to achieve the correct behavior of the movie. Sometimes I need to solve some equations or a complex math problem and once they're solved, I begin the ActionScript process. I turn on my PC, open Flash, and start turning my sketches into ActionScript.

I've been experimenting with masks a lot recently. Dynamic masks can be used to develop a lot of interesting visual effects, and since Flash 4, advanced Flash developers have coded draggable masks to create magnifying glasses, jigsaw puzzles, liquid images, and many other things. This was a bit complex because masks were not scriptable, so they had to learn a lot of tricks to solve these tasks.

Macromedia have added a lot of new ActionScript features in Flash MX. For instance we don't need to draw or insert movie clips on the stage. Now we can create all the necessary objects with code, which is pretty amazing. Best of all, dynamic masking in MX is so easy, we don't need to use the old Flash 4/5 tricks.

There is a lot of code in this chapter, so to save your tired fingers you can download all the source files from www.friendsofed.com.

Who is that masked man?

Not the Lone Ranger - but it could be - you can mask anything with the new setMask feature. Within the ActionScript Dictionary, you will see that:

> **"... Usage**
> myMovieClip.setMask (maskMovieClip)
>
> **Parameters**
> myMovieClip The instance name of a movie clip to be masked.
> maskMovieClip The instance name of a movie clip to be a mask.

I prefer to use this notation, because is self-explanatory.

```
masked.setMask (masker)
```

We define the movie clip that needs to be *masked* and the movie clip that will act as mask (*masker*). For instance we've got a movie clip (yellow square) that will be masked by a draggable movie clip (blue circle).

```
circle.startDrag(true);
square.setMask(circle);
```

before masking

after masking

The golden rules of dynamic masking

Rule 1: A masker movie clip can't be used to mask more than one object at the same time.

If we script like this:

```
masked1.setMask (masker)
masked2.setMask (masker)
masked3.setMask (masker)
```

...only `masked3` will be masked!

For example we have a draggable red circle over a yellow square and a green triangle. This piece of code doesn't work properly because only the yellow square is masked, as you can see in the second picture here.

```
circle.startDrag(true);
triangle.setMask(circle);
square.setMask(circle);
```

The solution is to nest both movie clips (the yellow square and green triangle) within a "holder" movie clip, as seen in the third right-hand picture.

```
circle.startDrag(true);
holder.setMask(circle);
```

no mask

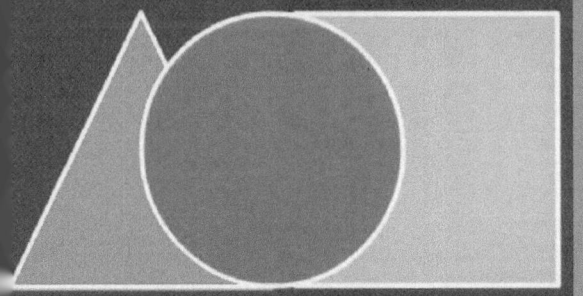

wrong mask

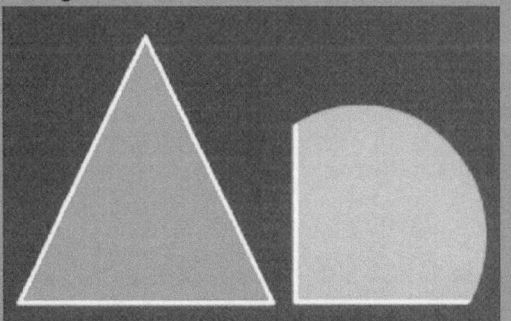

correct mask

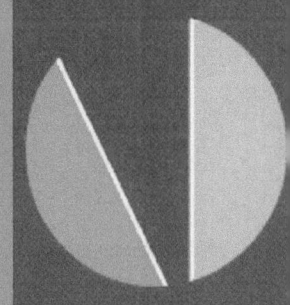

Rule 2: A movie clip can't be masked by more than one "masker" movie clip at the same time.

If our script looks like this:

```
masked.setMask (masker1)
masked.setMask (masker2)
masked.setMask (masker3)
```

...only `masker3` will act as a mask.

We have a red circle and a green triangle over a yellow square. If we try to use both shapes as maskers, only the last one will act as mask, as seen in the center image.

```
square.setMask(circle);
square.setMask(triangle);
```

If you need to use multiple movie clips as masks over the same movie clip, you can create a "holder" movie clip and then embed all the maskers, seen here in the image on the right.

```
square.setMask(holder);
```

no mask   **wrong mask**   **correct mask**

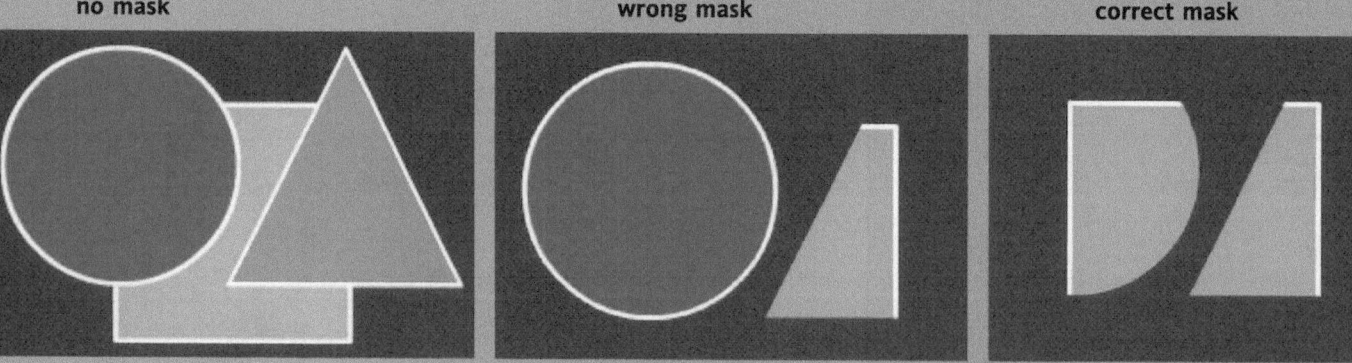

Rule 3: Drawing API lines or curves can't be used as masks.

Only filled drawing API shapes can be act as masks. Lines can't be changed to filled shapes so I have developed a method to draw filled lines and Bezier curves (This is explained in greater detail within my Drawing API chapter).

Rule 4; You can't mask an external image if it hasn't been loaded completely.

For instance this code doesn't work properly because the setMask function was called before the external image is on the stage.

```
holder.loadMovie("blue.jpg");
holder.setMask(mask);
mask.startDrag(true);
```

We need to include an image preloader; this way the setMask command will be called once the image has been loaded.

This piece of code will create a draggable square that will mask an external JPG image (named blue.jpg - you can use any you like, as long as it's in the same directory) after it's 100% loaded.

```
MovieClip.prototype.loader = function(file) {
    this.createEmptyMovieClip("image", 1);
    this.image.loadMovie(file);
    this.onEnterFrame = function() {
      if (this.image.getBytesLoaded() ==
➡this.image.getBytesTotal()&& this.image.getBytesTotal()>0) {
        this.image.setMask(mask);
        mask.startDrag(true);
        this.onEnterFrame = null;
      }
    };
};
MovieClip.prototype.drawBox = function(x, y, xsize, ysize,
strokewidth, strokecolor, strokealpha, fillcolor, fillalpha) {
    this.clear();
    this.beginFill(fillcolor, fillalpha);
    this.lineStyle(strokewidth, strokecolor, strokealpha);
    this.moveTo(x-xsize/2, y-ysize/2);
    this.lineTo(x+xsize/2, y-ysize/2);
    this.lineTo(x+xsize/2, y+ysize/2);
    this.lineTo(x-xsize/2, y+ysize/2);
    this.endFill();
};
this.createEmptyMovieClip("holder", 1);
this.createEmptyMovieClip("mask", 2);
this.mask.drawBox(0, 0, 100, 100, 0, 0xffffff, 100, 0x0000ff, 100);
holder.loader("blue.jpg");
stop();
```

Well, we've now got the foundations of dynamic masking covered, let's take a look at masks in action.

masking an external image without preloader

masking an external image with preloader

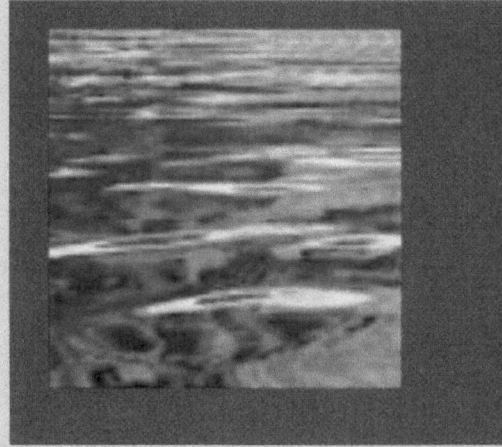

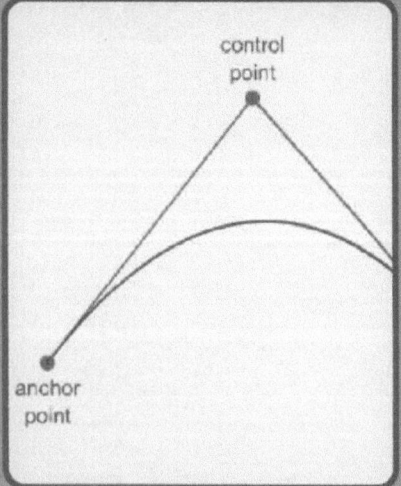

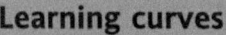

Learning curves

The purpose of these experiments is to prove that we can combine the new dynamic mask features with the drawing API methods. I'm also going to use the new event handlers and some object-oriented programming (OOP) concepts.

To this end, we're going to draw and animate some organic shapes, and then we are going to use these shapes as dynamic masks.

We'll use lines (lineTo) and curves (curveTo) to join some points. LineTo draws a straight line between two points, while curveTo draws a parabolic segment (quadratic Bezier spline) between two points (anchor points). The shape of the curve is controlled by a third external point named the control point.

Bezier splines are an interesting property: the slope of the Bezier curve at the anchor point and the slope of the straight line between the anchor point and the control point are the same.

These type of curves were developed by a French mathematician named Pierre Bézier, and will be the basis of our experiments.

Throwing shapes

First of all we need to learn a method or trick to soften a shape. For instance we've an irregular polygon with seven vertices and seven sides, and we want to draw a continuous curve that passes through the polygon. How?

First we calculate the midpoint of each side.

Then draw a number of Bezier curves, using each vertex as the control point and use the midpoints of the adjacent sides as the anchors.

As you can see, if we want a closed shape with *n* vertices, we must draw *n* Bezier curves.

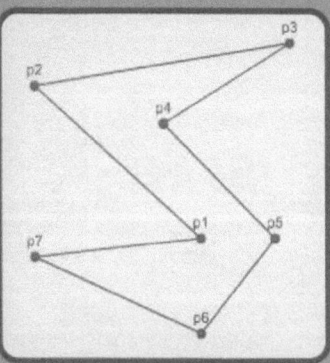
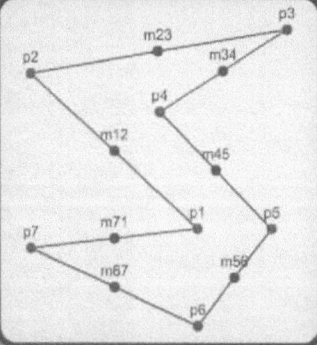
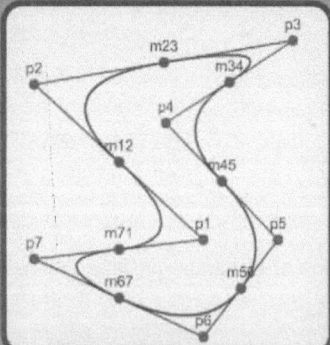
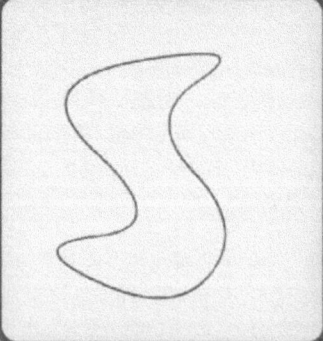

We can use the same idea to soften an open shape, but this time we must draw *n-2* Bezier curves. For instance, we've got an open shape with nine vertices and eight sides – the procedure is the same, except that the extreme vertices (p1 and p9) are used as anchor points instead of the midponts of the extreme sides (m12 and m89) that are not used.

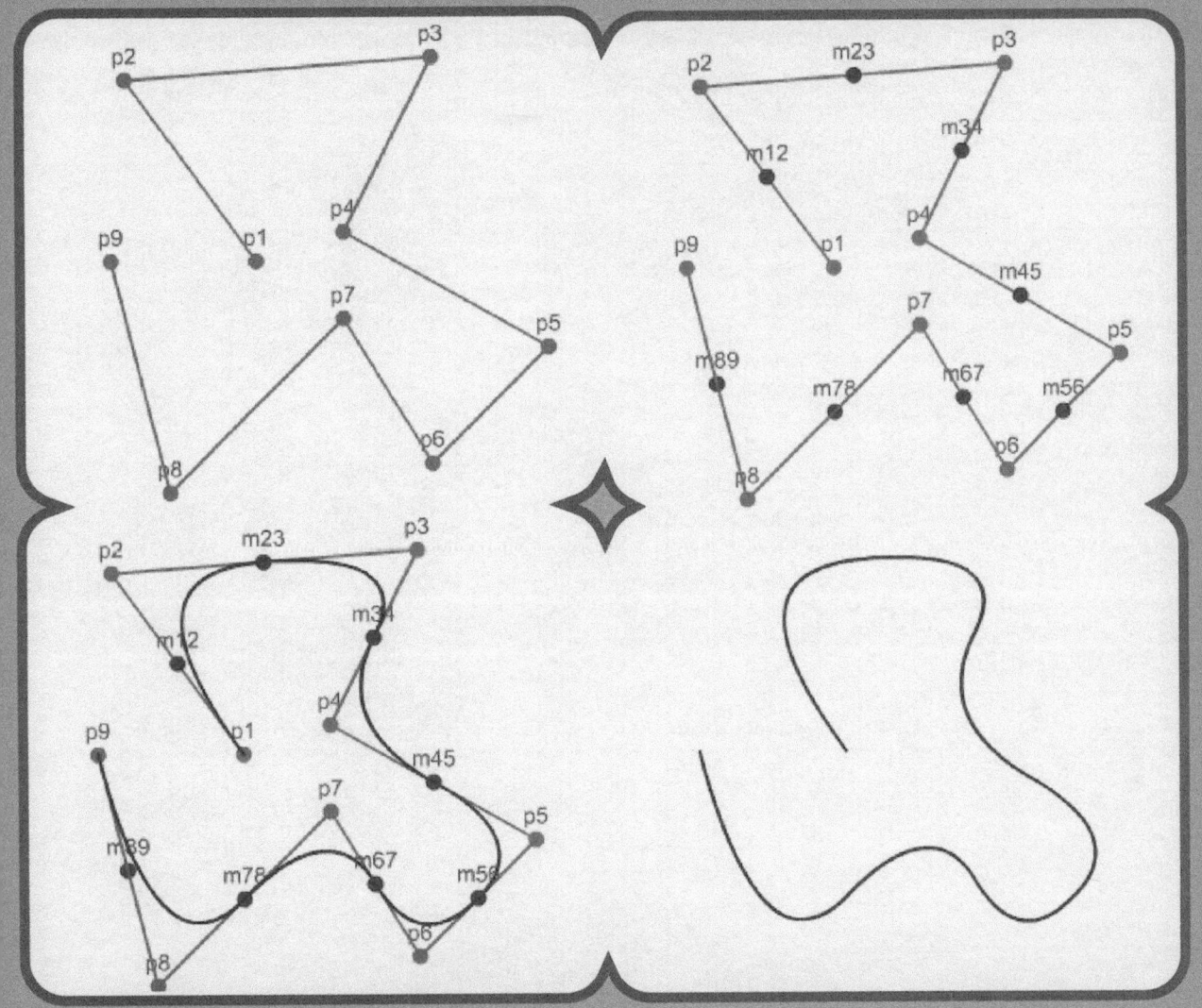

It's really easy!

You can appreciate that there are neither corners nor discontinuities, so the curve is smooth, soft, organic...

Try drawing complex shapes in order to assimilate this method. If you are an advanced math developer, try coding a 3D version of this Bezier spline. The method is the same, although you will need to use x, y, z triplets to define each point.

Bezier waves

I want to simulate waving horizontal surfaces, but I also want movement, motion, something like the waves of the sea. The solution could be defining some points, that will move softly up and down, and then drawing straight lines or Bezier curves between them.

The vertical position of each point will be modulated at a random amplitude and frequency, so every time we've got a different result.

Code and file structure

I usually include all the functions and methods within the first frame, while the second frame is used to define variables, creating objects and to set up the onEnterFrame loop. I keep the functions and methods definitons stored on the first frame, and perforrm all of the calls on the second frame. I use this file structure just for order and because it is easy to read and debug (if you'd like, you can put all the code within the first frame).

I'm going to create, at first, a starting point with the firs piece of code, and then in the proceeding versions of th experiments I'm going to show variations, just adding o removing some lines of code or changing some variables o the second frame.

Remember that I have included all the source files, so ope the mx_bezier_waves_01.fla file and follow me.

The first step is to develop an OOP wave class using constructor function. Within the constructor we define a the properties of our wave, the number of points, radiu (amplitude), x, y position, etc. Each "wave object" has "bodyholder" movie clip, that holds all of the graphica elements.

mx_bezier_waves_01

This is the ActionScript in the first frame:

```
function wave(points, radius, offset, wavewidth, xpos, ypos, strokewidth,
strokecolor, strokealpha, fillcolor, fillalpha) {
   this.body = createEmptyMovieClip("bodyholder"+k, 1000+k++);
   this.x = [];      // this array holds the horizontal position of each point
   this.y = [];      // this array holds the vertical position of each point
   this.mx = [];     //this array holds the horizontal position of each midpoint
   this.my = [];     //this array holds the vertical position of each midpoint
   this.frec = [];   //this array holds the modulation frequency of each point
   this.wavewidth = wavewidth;
   this.xpos = xpos;
   this.ypos = ypos;
   this.radius = radius;
   this.offset = offset;
   this.points = points;
   this.strokewidth = strokewidth;
   this.strokecolor = strokecolor;
   this.strokealpha = strokealpha;
   this.fillcolor = fillcolor;
   this.fillalpha = fillalpha;
   for (var i = 0; i<points; i++) {
       this.frec[i] = 1.2*(Math.random()+.5);
   }
}
```

..then we define the following methods:

This one modifies the vertical value of each point, generating a sinusoidal movement. So every time we call this method, the new coordinates of the points (x,y) and midpoints (mx,my) are calculated:

```
this.wave.prototype.modulate = function(t) {
    for (var i = 0; i<this.points; i++) {
      this.x[i] = this.xpos+(this.wavewidth/(this.points-1))*i;
      this.y[i] = this.ypos+this.radius+this.offset*Math.sin(this.frec[i]*t*dtr);
      this.mx[i] = (this.x[i]+this.x[i-1])/2;
      this.my[i] = (this.y[i]+this.y[i-1])/2;
    }
};
```

This method draws straight lines between each adjacent point or vertex of our shape. As you can see we are using some drawing API methods to draw lines and fill surfaces.

```
this.wave.prototype.drawLines = function() {
    this.body.beginFill(this.fillcolor, this.fillalpha);
    this.body.lineStyle(this.strokewidth, this.strokecolor, this.strokealpha);
    this.body.moveTo(this.xpos, this.ypos);
    this.body.lineTo(this.x[0], this.y[0]);
    for (var i = 1; i<this.points; i++) {
      this.body.lineTo(this.x[i], this.y[i]);
    }
    this.body.lineTo(this.x[this.points-1], this.ypos);
    this.body.endFill();
};
```

This method, which is similar, draws Bezier curves between each vertex and its adjacent midpoints. We can see the smoothing method in action.

```
this.wave.prototype.drawCurves = function() {
    this.body.beginFill(this.fillcolor, this.fillalpha);
    this.body.lineStyle(this.strokewidth, this.strokecolor, this.strokealpha);
    this.body.moveTo(this.xpos, this.ypos);
    this.body.lineTo(this.x[0], this.y[0]);
    for (var i = 1; i<this.points-2; i++) {
      this.body.curveTo(this.x[i], this.y[i], this.mx[i+1], this.my[i+1]);
    }
    this.body.curveTo(this.x[this.points-2], this.y[this.points-2],
    this.x[this.points-1], this.y[this.points-1]);
    this.body.lineTo(this.x[this.points-1], this.ypos);
    this.body.endFill();
};
```

In my FLA this ActionScript lives on the second frame.. Finally we define some variables, create a movie clip to hold the image and generate our first "wave" object. The onEnterFrame event handler allows the wave movement.

Keep in mind that we're now dealing with a FLA file where the JPG image is an object in our library and is attached with the `attachMovie` command.

```
dtr = Math.PI/180;                  //degrees to radians conversion factor
speed = 5;//modulation speed
sx = Stage.width/2;                 // stage horizontal center
sy = Stage.height/2;                // stage vertical center
wave[1] = new wave(10, -2*Stage.height/4, 30, Stage.width, 0,
➥ Stage.height, 2, 0xffffff, 100, 0x6633ff, 100);
createEmptyMovieClip("image", 1);
image.attachMovie("image01", "img", 1);
image._x=sx;
image._y=sy;
image.setMask(wave[1].body);
this.onEnterFrame = function() {
    wave[1].modulate(speed*fa++);
    wave[1].body.clear();
    wave[1].drawLines();
};
stop();
```

You can appreciate that `wave[1]` has 10 points, the fixed size is 2/4 of the stage height, the variable vertical offset is 30, the horizontal wave size is equal to the stage width and the bottom left corner of the wave is located at the bottom left corner of the stage.

This line of code is used to make the dynamic mask effect:

```
image.setMask(wave[1].body);
```

mx_bezier_waves_02

Now we want to draw curves instead of straight lines, so use `drawCurves` instead of the `drawLines` method and compare both results. In this FLA the `onEnterFrame` function becomes:

```
this.onEnterFrame = function() {
    wave[1].modulate(speed*fa++);
    wave[1].body.clear();
    wave[1].drawCurves();
};
```

...as you can see, the wave movement is better; very "liquid" and much more real, because there are no corners.

You can modify these parameters in order to obtain different shapes:

points = number of points or vertices of the wave
radius = fixed vertical value of the points
offset= variable vertical value of the points
wavewidth = horizontal wave size
xpos= horizontal position of the bottom left corner of the wave
ypos= vertical position of the bottom left corner of the wave
strokewidth, strokecolor, strokealpha, fillcolor, and fillalpha are self
explanatory

mx_bezier_waves_03

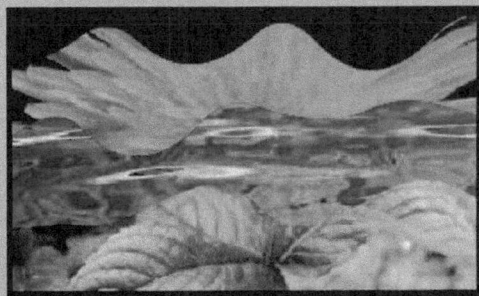

For this experiment, I'm drawing 3 waves, arranged in a vertical order, and each wave
will be masking its own image. Remember that we are using the same body of the
code, so we don't need to rewrite all again. Just modify the head.

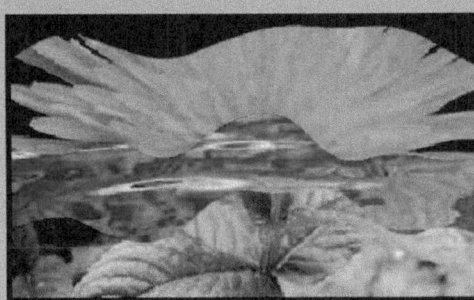

```
dtr = Math.PI/180;          //degrees to radians conversion factor
speed = 5;//modulation speed
sx = Stage.width/2;      // stage horizontal center
sy = Stage.height/2;     // stage vertical center
imageArray = ["image01", "image02", "image03"];
                             // array of linked images names
image = [];                  // array of image holders
for (var i = 0; i<3; i++) {
    wave[i] = new wave(10, (i-3)*Stage.height/4, 20,
➡ Stage.width, 0, Stage.height, 2, 0xffffff, 100, 0x6633ff, 100);
    image[i] = createEmptyMovieClip("image"+i, i);
    image[i].attachMovie(imageArray[i], "img", 1);
    image[i]._x=sx,
    image[i]._y=sy;
    image[i].setMask(wave[i].body);
}
this.onEnterFrame = function() {
    for (var i = 0; i<3; i++) {
      wave[i].modulate(speed*fa++);
      wave[i].body.clear();
      wave[i].drawCurves();
    }
};
```

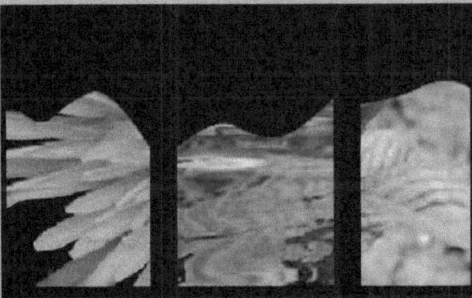

Each linked image needs a holder, so we generate these movie clips using
createEmptyMovieClip method.

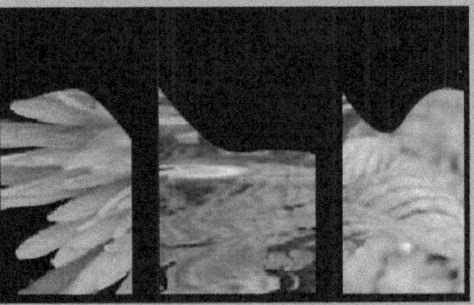

This time we've got 3 waves arranged in an horizontal order, side by side:

```
dtr = Math.PI/180;          //degrees to radians conversion factor
speed = 5;//modulation speed
sx = Stage.width/2;      // stage horizontal center
sy = Stage.height/2;     // stage vertical center
// array of linked images names
imageArray = ["image01", "image02", "image03"];
image = [];// array of image holders
```

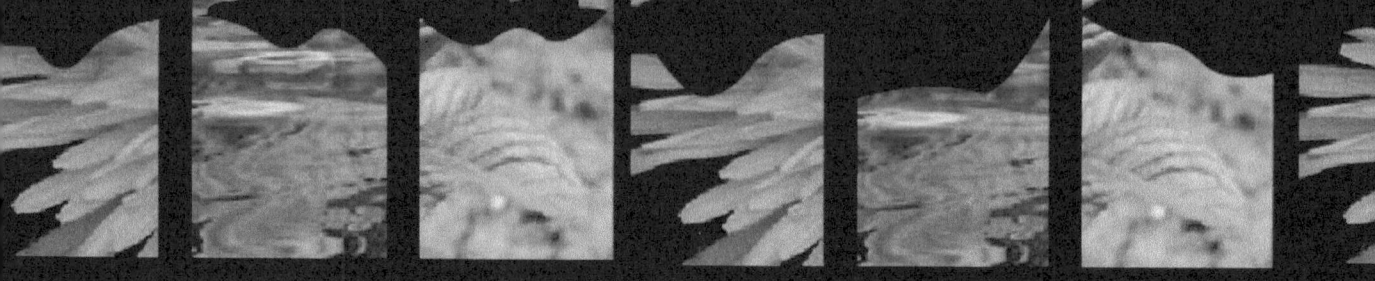

```
for (var i = 0; i<3; i++) {
    wave[i] = new wave(5, -.5*Stage.height, 20, Stage.width/3.5, i*Stage.width/3,
    ➡ Stage.height, 2, 0xffffff, 100, 0x6633ff, 100);
    image[i] = createEmptyMovieClip("image"+i, i);
    image[i].attachMovie(imageArray[i], "img", 1);
    image[i]._x=sx, image[i]._y=sy;
    image[i].setMask(wave[i].body);
}
this.onEnterFrame = function() {
    for (var i = 0; i<3; i++) {
        wave[i].modulate(speed*fa++);
        wave[i].body.clear();
        wave[i].drawCurves();
    }
};
```

mx_bezier_waves_05

This time I'm using 3 couples of waves, so we need to create 6 waves. Each wave is opposed to the other, so we get inter-esting double sided waves. I'm masking just one image, so I embed all the waves into a holder movie clip, named 'multiple'.

```
dtr = Math.PI/180,speed = 5;
sx = Stage.width/2, sy = Stage.height/2;
this.multiple = createEmptyMovieClip("mult", 50);
wave[0] = new wave(21, -.05*Stage.height, .047*Stage.height, Stage.width, 0,
➡ Stage.height/4, 2, 0xffffff, 100, 0x6633ff, 100);
wave[1] = new wave(21, .05*Stage.height, .047*Stage.height, Stage.width, 0,
➡ Stage.height/4, 2, 0xffffff, 100, 0x6633ff, 100);
wave[2] = new wave(21, -.05*Stage.height, .047*Stage.height, Stage.width,
➡ 0, 2*Stage.height/4, 2, 0xffffff, 100, 0x6633ff, 100);
wave[3] = new wave(21, .05*Stage.height, .047*Stage.height, Stage.width, 0,
➡ 2*Stage.height/4, 2, 0xffffff, 100, 0x6633ff, 100);
wave[4] = new wave(21, -.05*Stage.height, .047*Stage.height, Stage.width, 0, ➡
➡3*Stage.height/4, 2, 0xffffff, 100, 0x6633ff, 100);
wave[5] = new wave(21, .05*Stage.height, .047*Stage.height, Stage.width, 0, 3*Stage.height/4,
➡ 2, 0xffffff, 100, 0x6633ff, 100);
image = createEmptyMovieClip("image", i);
image.attachMovie("image01", "img", 1);
image._x=sx, image._y=sy;
image.setMask(multiple);
this.onEnterFrame = function() {
    for (var i = 0; i<6; i++) {
        wave[i].modulate(speed*fa++);
        wave[i].body.clear();
        wave[i].drawCurves();
    }
```

We also need to change just one line of code within the constructor function:

```
this.body = multiple.createEmptyMovieClip("bodyholder"+k, 1000+k++);
```

The result is a nice piece of abstract art!

You can easily modify a lot of parameters, such as the wave size, position, speed, amplitude, and so on, so there are millions of combinations. This is the magic of OOP programming!

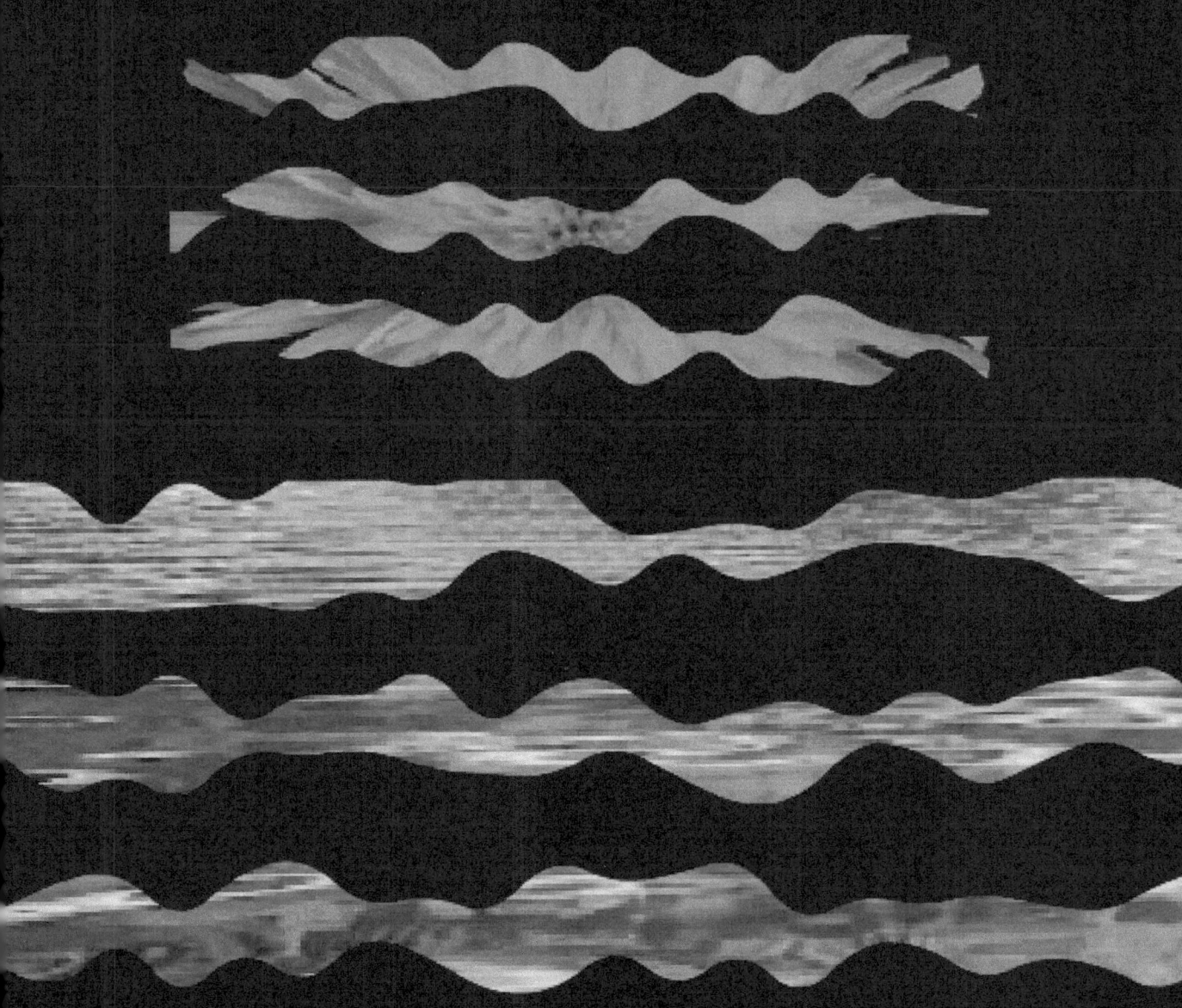

Bezier amoebas

These creatures are very nice. This time we use a radial pattern to plot the points, so the shape looks like a undulating amoeba or something like that.

Again, the radius of each point will be modulated at a random amplitude and frequency. The procedure is pretty similar to the former experiment. Once the functions and methods are in place, we can benerate a lot of variations just by changing the parameters in frame 2.

mx_bezier_amoeba_01

Firstly we need to create a constructor function in order to define all the object properties.

```
function amoeba(points, radius, offset, xpos, ypos, strokewidth, stroke
➥ color, strokealpha, fillcolor, fillalpha) {
   this.body = createEmptyMovieClip("bodyholder"+k, 1000+ k++);
   this.x = [];
   this.y = [];
   this.mx = [];
   this.my = [];
   this.xpos = xpos;
   this.ypos = ypos;
   this.radius = radius;
   this.offset = offset;
   this.frec = [];
   this.points = points;
   this.strokewidth = strokewidth;
   this.strokecolor = strokecolor;
   this.strokealpha = strokealpha;
   this.fillcolor = fillcolor;
   this.fillalpha = fillalpha;
   for (var i = 0; i<points; i++) {
     this.frec[i] = 2*(Math.random()+.5);
   }
 }
```

...then we define a few other amoeba methods:

This one is to modify the radial value of each point, generating a sinusoidal movement. Here we must calculate the x and y position of each point, according to its angle.

```
this.amoeba.prototype.modulate = function(t) {
   for (var i = 0; i<this.points; i++) {
     var ran = this.radius+this.offset*Math.sin(this.frec[i]*t*dtr);
     this.x[i] = this.xpos+ran*Math.cos(i*2*Math.PI/this.points);
     this.y[i] = this.ypos+ran*Math.sin(i*2*Math.PI/this.points);
     this.mx[i] = (this.x[i]+this.x[i-1])/2;
     this.my[i] = (this.y[i]+this.y[i-1])/2;
   }
   this.mx[0] = (this.x[this.points-1]+this.x[0])/2;
   this.my[0] = (this.y[this.points-1]+this.y[0])/2;
 };
```

The `drawCurves` method, will draw Bezier curves between each vertex and its adjacent midpoints, just applying the same smoothing method as we have before:

```
this.amoeba.prototype.drawCurves = function() {
    this.body.clear();
    this.body.beginFill(this.fillcolor, this.fillalpha);
    this.body.lineStyle(this.strokewidth,
    ➥this.strokecolor, this.strokealpha);
    this.body.moveTo(this.mx[0], this.my[0]);
    for (var i = 0; i<this.points-1; i++) {
      this.body.curveTo(this.x[i], this.y[i], this.mx[i+1], this.my[i+1]);
    }
    this.body.curveTo(this.x[this.points-1], this.y[this.points-1], this.mx[0],
    ➥ this.my[0]);
    this.body.endFill();
};
```

This method is to draw lines between each adjacent point or vertex:

```
this.amoeba.prototype.drawLines = function() {
    this.body.beginFill(this.fillcolor, this.fillalpha);
    this.body.lineStyle(this.strokewidth, this.strokecolor, this.strokeal-
pha);
    this.body.moveTo(this.x[0], this.y[0]);
    for (var i = 1; i<this.points-1; i++) {
      this.body.lineTo(this.x[i], this.y[i]);
    }
    this.body.lineTo(this.x[0], this.y[0]);
    this.body.endFill();
};
```

After defining the class constructor and its methods, we generate our first artificial amoeba. This amoeba has 21 points, and is located at the center of the movie stage. You can see that I'm using straight lines between adjacent points.

```
dtr=Math.PI/180, speed=5, sx=Stage.width/2, sy=Stage.height/2;
amoeba[1] = new amoeba(21, Stage.height/2.5, Stage.height/15,
➥ Stage.width/2, Stage.height/2, 2, 0xffffff, 100, 0x6633ff, 100);
createEmptyMovieClip("image", 1);
image.attachMovie("image01", "img", 1);
image._x=sx, image._y=sy;
image.setMask(amoeba[1].body);
this.onEnterFrame = function() {
    amoeba[1].modulate(speed*fa++);
    amoeba[1].body.clear();
    amoeba[1].drawLines();
};
stop();
```

We need just one line of code to set up the mask:

```
this.image01.setMask(amoeba[1].body);
```

The `onEnterFrame` event handler allows the amoeba movement. The key variables, which you can alter to mess with the effect, are:

`points` =number of points or vertices
`radius` = fixed radial value
`offset`= variable radial value
`xpos`= horizontal position of the amoeba center
`ypos`= vertical position of the amoeba center
`strokewidth`, `strokecolor`, `strokealpha`, `fillcolor`, and `fillalpha` are self explanatory

Now it's time to play by changing some values in order to generate different kinds of effects.

mx_bezier_amoeba_02

We have the same object configuration, but this time we use the `drawCurves` method in order to draw soft curves between adjacent points.

```
this.onEnterFrame = function() {
    amoeba[1].modulate(speed*fa++);
    amoeba[1].body.clear();
    amoeba[1].drawCurves();
};
```

mx_bezier_amoeba_03

Our amoeba is dynamic but lacking in interactivity, so I'm going to change the offset value according to the mouse distance. Add this piece of code within the body of the code (first frame). This new method returns the distance between the mouse and the amoeba's center.

```
this.amoeba.prototype.distance = function() {
    var dx = _xmouse-this.xpos,
    var dy = _ymouse-this.ypos;
    return Math.sqrt(dx*dx+dy*dy);
};
```

Within the `onEnterFrame` event handler, I have defined an exponential relation to set the modulation offset. The result is very interesting; the amoeba reacts to mouse proximity.

```
this.onEnterFrame = function() {
    amoeba[1].offset = 25*Math.exp(-(
    ➡ amoeba[1].distance())/50);
    amoeba[1].modulate(speed*fa++);
```

```
amoeba[1].body.clear();
amoeba[1].drawCurves();
};
```

mx_bezier_amoeba_04

This time I'm going to generate a bi-dimensional array of amoebas. Each one will react to mouse proximity. I need to mask just one image, so I've embedded all the amoebas' bodies into a holder movie clip, named "multiple".

```
dtr=Math.PI/180, speed=2, sx=Stage.width/
➡ 2, sy=Stage.height/2;
createEmptyMovieClip("image", 1);
image.attachMovie("image01", "img", 1);
image._x=sx, image._y=sy;
multiple = createEmptyMovieClip("mult", 50);
rows=4;
columns=6;
for (var i = 0; i<rows; i++) {
    amoeba[i] = [];
    for (var j = 0; j<columns; j++) {
        amoeba[i][j] = new amoeba(4, 25, 7,
        ➡ (j+1)*Stage.width/(columns+1),
        ➡ (i+1)*Stage.height/(rows+1), 2,
        ➡ 0xffffff, 100, 0x6633ff, 100);
    }
}
image.setMask(multiple);
this.onEnterFrame = function() {
    for (var i = 0; i<rows; i++) {
        for (var j = 0; j<columns; j++) {
            amoeba[i][j].offset = 25*Math.exp(-
            ➡ amoeba[i][j].distance()/50);
            amoeba[i][j].modulate(speed*fa++);
            amoeba[i][j].body.clear();
            amoeba[i][j].drawCurves();
        }
    }
};
stop();
```

We also need to change just one line of code within the 'constructor' function:

```
this.body = multiple.createEmptyMovieClip("body
➡ holder"+k, k++);
```

...you can also change the number of rows and columns in order to obtain other visual patterns. Use lower numbers if your processor is slow.

mx_bezier_amoeba_05

The amoeba will follow the mouse and the masked image will change dynamically when you press over the amoeba.

```
dtr=Math.PI/180, speed=2, sx=Stage.width/2,
sy=Stage.height/2, easing=.1;
image._x=sx, image._y=sy;
imageArray = ["image01", "image02", "image03"];
image = [];
for (var i = 0; i<3; i++) {
    image[i] = createEmptyMovieClip("image"+i, 3-i);
    image[i].attachMovie(imageArray[i], "img", 1);
    image[i]._x=sx, image[i]._y=sy;
}
amoeba[1] = new amoeba(15, 50, 15, Stage.width/2,
Stage.height/2, 2, 0xffffff, 100, 0x6633ff, 100);
image[0].setMask(amoeba[1].body);
this.onEnterFrame = function() {
    amoeba[1].move((1-easing)*amoeba[1].xpos+easing*_xmouse,
(1-easing)*amoeba[1].ypos+easing*_ymouse);
    amoeba[1].modulate(speed*fa++);
    amoeba[1].body.clear();
    amoeba[1].drawCurves();
};
amoeba[1].body.onPress = function() {
    d == 2 ? d=0 : d++;
    image[d].swapDepths(1000+dd++);
    image[d].setMask(amoeba[1].body);
};
stop();
```

We also include this new method:

```
this.amoeba.prototype.move = function(x, y) {
    this.xpos = x;
    this.ypos = y;
};
```

You can add or remove images as you want, just change the image array.

[2]

[3]

4 rows, 6 columns

[4]

2 rows, 3 columns

[4b]

[5a]

[5b] 7

mx_bezier_amoeba_06

Finally we've got a new kind of shape, like a ring. This amoeba looks like a ring or "aura". We have added a new parameter: circle radius that can be internal or external. I have modified the class constructor and methods so I need to write some new code.

We have added the x, y coordinates of the internal circle points (ix, iy) and its midpoints (imx,imy):

```
function amoeba(points, radius, offset, innerradius, xpos, ypos, strokewidth, strokecolor,
strokealpha, fillcolor, fillalpha) {
    this.body = createEmptyMovieClip("mybody"+k, 1000+k++);
    this.x=[], this.y=[], this.mx=[], this.my=[];
    this.ix=[], this.iy=[], this.imx=[], this.imy=[];
    this.innerradius = innerradius;
    this.xpos=xpos, this.ypos=ypos;
    this.radius=radius, this.offset=offset, this.frec=[], this.points=points;
    this.strokewidth=strokewidth, this.strokecolor=strokecolor, this.strokealpha=strokealpha,
    ➡ this.fillcolor=fillcolor, this.fillalpha=fillalpha;
    for (var i = 0; i<points; i++) {
        this.frec[i] = 2*(Math.random()+.5);
    }
}
```

This time the modulate method calculates the location of the inner circle points and midpoints too.

```
this.amoeba.prototype.modulate = function(t) {
    for (var i = 0; i<this.points; i++) {
        var ran = this.radius+this.offset*Math.sin(this.frec[i]*t*dtr);
        this.x[i] = this.xpos+ran*Math.cos(i*2*Math.PI/this.points);
        this.y[i] = this.ypos+ran*Math.sin(i*2*Math.PI/this.points);
        this.mx[i] = (this.x[i]+this.x[i-1])/2;
        this.my[i] = (this.y[i]+this.y[i-1])/2;
        var r = this.innerradius;
        this.ix[i] = this.xpos+r*Math.cos(i*2*Math.PI/this.points);
        this.iy[i] = this.ypos+r*Math.sin(i*2*Math.PI/this.points);
        this.imx[i] = (this.ix[i]+this.ix[i-1])/2;
        this.imy[i] = (this.iy[i]+this.iy[i-1])/2;
    }
    this.mx[0] = (this.x[this.points-1]+this.x[0])/2;
    this.my[0] = (this.y[this.points-1]+this.y[0])/2;
    this.imx[0] = (this.ix[this.points-1]+this.ix[0])/2;
    this.imy[0] = (this.iy[this.points-1]+this.iy[0])/2;
};
```

I have also modified the drawCurves method. As you can see it is not easy drawing a filled ring to use as a mask.

```
this.amoeba.prototype.drawCurves = function() {
    this.body.clear();
    this.body.beginFill(this.fillcolor, this.fillalpha);
    this.body.lineStyle(this.strokewidth, this.strokecolor, this.stroke
    ➡ this.body.moveTo(this.imx[0], this.imy[0]);
```

```
  this.body.curveTo(this.ix[this.points-1], this.iy[this.points-1], this.imx[this.points-1],
  ➥ this.imy[this.points-1]);
  for (var i = this.points-2; i>=0; i—) {
    this.body.curveTo(this.ix[i], this.iy[i], this.imx[i], this.imy[i]);
  }
  this.body.lineTo(this.mx[0], this.my[0]);
  for (var i = 0; i<=this.points-2; i++) {
    this.body.curveTo(this.x[i], this.y[i], this.mx[i+1], this.my[i+1]);
  }
  this.body.curveTo(this.x[this.points-1], this.y[this.points-1], this.mx[0], this.my[0]);
  this.body.lineTo(this.imx[0], this.imy[0]);
  this.body.endFill();
};
```

...and finally we create a couple of Bezier auras for the ring. .The big one has an inner fixed radius while the little one has an outer fixed radius (fig.21).

```
dtr=Math.PI/180, speed=2, sx=Stage.width/2, sy=Stage.height/2, easing=.1;
image._x=sx, image._y=sy;
imageArray = ["image03", "image02", "image01"];
image = [];
amoeba[0] = new amoeba(30, .15*Stage.height, .09*Stage.height, .25*Stage.height, Stage.width/2,
➥ Stage.height/2, 2, 0xffffff, 100, 0x6633ff, 100);
amoeba[1] = new amoeba(30, .45*Stage.height, .09*Stage.height, .35*Stage.height, Stage.width/2,
➥ Stage.height/2, 2, 0xffffff, 100, 0x6633ff, 100);
for (var i = 0; i<3; i++) {
    image[i] = createEmptyMovieClip("image"+i, 3-i);
    image[i].attachMovie(imageArray[i], "img", 1);
    image[i]._x=sx, image[i]._y=sy;
}
image[0].setMask(amoeba[0].body);
image[1].setMask(amoeba[1].body);
this.onEnterFrame = function() {
    for (var i = 0; i<2; i++) {
        amoeba[i].modulate(speed*fa++);
        amoeba[i].body.clear();
        amoeba[i].drawCurves();
    }
};
stop();
```

hat's all, so go be creative and discover your own new Bezier shapes.

m sure by now you've learned a lot about the new dynamic mask functions and its unlimited posibilities. These examples may ot be the most useful, but are useful for illustrating a lot of the new Flash MX ActionScript functions.

Image explosion

The purpose of this application is to show that we can break an image into a lot of small pieces in order to make some nice transition effects. This will be achieved using the power of dynamic masks (no more motion tweening or static masks!)

First of all, there is an image on the stage that I want to destroy, smashing it into small shards, so each and every time the pattern will have a different look. When this happens, each piece will be broken into smaller pieces – by a random fractal process dependent on a set number of fractal levels.

Again, don't use more than 3 levels if you have a slow processor.

This is an OOP project, so the first step is to define our 'piece' class constructor function:

mx_explosion_01

This is the body script - entered in the first frame. You can see that this function receives the x, y coordinates of each vertex of the triangle, the fractal level and some drawing API values as parameters.

```
function piece(x1, y1, x2, y2, x3, y3, level) {
    this.initTriangle(x1, y1, x2, y2, x3, y3, level);
    this.drawTriangle();
    this.body.level<maxlevel ? this.loopFractalTriangle() : null;
}
```

Now to add some of the fundfamental methods. This method will be used to set some properties of the body of the piece. The body is a movie clip that holds all the graphic elements of the object...

Inside the body movie clip, we've got 2 movie clips: the movie clip named 'masked' will be masked by movie clip named 'masker' (that should be obvious). `masked` holds the JPG image that is embedded via `attachMovie`, while masker holds the shape that will be drawn using the drawing API. Keep in mind that this time we are using a triangular shape, so we've got just 3 vertice (x1,y1), (x2,y2) and (x3,y3). The center of each triangle will be the baricenter (or gravity center) (x4,y4). We also perform som movements in order to set the baricenter as the movie clip x,y origin of each triangle.

We then apply some random color transformation to every triangle shape.

```
this.piece.prototype.initTriangle = function(x1, y1, x2, y2, x3, y3, level) {
    this.body = createEmptyMovieClip("bodyholder"+k, 1000+k++);
    this.body.level = level;
    this.body.ref = this;
    this.body.x1=x1, this.body.x2=x2, this.body.x3=x3, this.body.x4=(x1+x2+x3)/3;
    this.body.y1=y1, this.body.y2=y2, this.body.y3=y3, this.body.y4=(y1+y2+y3)/3;
    this.body.masked = this.body.createEmptyMovieClip("masked", 1);
    this.body.masker = this.body.createEmptyMovieClip("masker", 2);
    this.body.masked.attachMovie("image01", "img", 1);
    this.body.masked._x = sx-this.body.x4;
    this.body.masked._y = sy-this.body.y4;
    this.body.masked.setMask(this.body.masker);
    this.mycolor = new Color(this.body);
    this.ran = 200*(Math.random()-.5);
    this.mycolor.setTransform({ra:100, rb:this.ran, ga:100, gb:this.ran,
    ➥ ba:100, bb:this.ran, aa:100, ab:0});
    this.body._x = this.body.x4;
    this.body._y = this.body.y4;
};
```

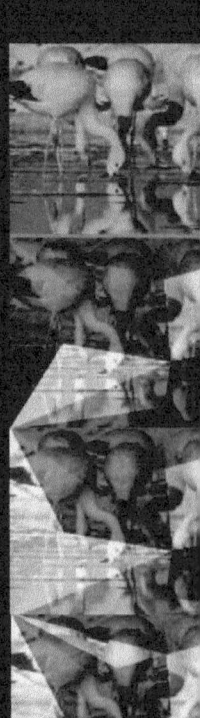

This method divides each triangle into three smaller triangles. We've got a conditional switch statement inside the `onEnterFrame` event handler in order to add color effects and some time delay between every triangle creation.

```
this.piece.prototype.loopFractalTriangle = function() {
  var counter = 0;
  this.body.onEnterFrame = function() {
    switch (counter) {
    case 1 :
      this.ref.mycolor.setTransform({ra:150, rb:this.ref.ran, ga:150, gb:this.ref.ran, ba:150,
bb:this.ref.ran, aa:100, ab:0});
      break;
    case 2 :
      this.ref.mycolor.setTransform({ra:100, rb:this.ref.ran, ga:100, gb:this.ref.ran, ba:100,
bb:this.ref.ran, aa:100, ab:0});
      break;
    case 3 :
      t[kk++] = new piece(this.x1, this.y1, this.x4, this.y4, this.x2, this.y2, this.level+1);
      break;
    case 5 :
      t[kk++] = new piece(this.x2, this.y2, this.x4, this.y4, this.x3, this.y3, this.level+1);
      break;
    case 7 :
      t[kk++] = new piece(this.x3, this.y3, this.x4, this.y4, this.x1, this.y1, this.level+1);
      break;
    case 9 :
      delete this.ref;
      this.removeMovieClip();
      break;
    }
    counter++;
  };
};
```

This method, `drawTriangle`, is just used to draw the triangle inside our masker movie clip, using some drawing API functions...

```
this.piece.prototype.drawTriangle = function() {
  this.body.masker.beginFill(0x000000, 100);
  this.body.masker.lineStyle(0, 0xffffff, 100);
  this.body.masker.moveTo(this.body.x1-this.body.x4, this.body.y1-this.body.y4);
  this.body.masker.lineTo(this.body.x2-this.body.x4, this.body.y2-this.body.y4);
  this.body.masker.lineTo(this.body.x3-this.body.x4, this.body.y3-this.body.y4);
  this.body.masker.lineTo(this.body.x1-this.body.x4, this.body.y1-this.body.y4);
  this.body.masker.endFill();
};
```

`newBox`: this method is used to draw a box on the stage that can be used as button.

```
MovieClip.prototype.newBox = function(xpos, ypos, mywidth, myheight, mytext, textsize,
➥ textcolor, textfont, textalign, strokewidth, strokecolor, strokealpha, fillcolor, fillalpha) {
  this.beginFill(fillcolor, fillalpha);
  this.lineStyle(strokewidth, strokecolor, strokealpha);
  this.moveTo(xpos-mywidth/2, ypos+myheight/2);
  this.lineTo(xpos-mywidth/2, ypos-myheight/2);
  this.lineTo(xpos+mywidth/2, ypos-myheight/2);
```

```
    this.lineTo(xpos+mywidth/2, ypos+myheight/2);
    this.endFill();
    this.createTextField("textum", 1, xpos-mywidth/2, ypos-myheight/2, mywidth, myheight);
    this.textum.text = mytext;
    this.myformat = new TextFormat();
    this.myformat.color = textcolor;
    this.myformat.font = textfont;
    this.myformat.align = textalign;
    this.myformat.size = textsize;
    this.textum.setTextFormat(this.myformat);
};
```

Finally, on the second frame, we define some variables and create the objects. The full image will be located at the center of the stage (sx,sy). We create a box that will be used as a button via an onPress event handler. Once pressed, the image will be divided into four triangles, where the corners and the center of the image are the vertex of the triangles. Well, the center (x0,y0) is not exactly the image center, because we are adding a random vector (r, angle) to the center coordinates (sx,sy).

```
maxlevel = 3;                          // number of fractal levels
dtr = Math.PI/180;                     // grades to radians conversion factor
sx = Stage.width/2;                    // stage horizontal center
sy = Stage.height/2;                   // stage vertical center
r = 20+30*Math.random();
angle = 360*Math.random();
rx = r*Math.cos(angle*dtr);
ry = r*Math.sin(angle*dtr);
x0=sx+rx, y0=sy+ry;                     // random center coordinates
this.createEmptyMovieClip("img", 1);
img.attachMovie("image01", "image", 1);
iw=img._width/2, ih=img._height/2;     // image center coordinates
img._x=sx, img._y=sy;
t = [];                                // objects array
createEmptyMovieClip("but01", 2);
but01.newBox(sx, sy+ih+30, 90, 20, "break", 14, 0xffffff, "arial", "center", 1, 0xffffff, 100,
0x999999, 100);
this.but01.onPress = function() {
    but01._visible=0;
    img._visible=0;
    t[kk++] = new piece(sx-iw, sy+ih, x0, y0, sx-iw, sy-ih, 1);
    t[kk++] = new piece(sx-iw, sy-ih, x0, y0, sx+iw, sy-ih, 1);
    t[kk++] = new piece(sx+iw, sy-ih, x0, y0, sx+iw, sy+ih, 1);
    t[kk++] = new piece(sx+iw, sy+ih, x0, y0, sx-iw, sy+ih, 1);
};
stop();
```

mx_explosion_02

We are going to modify the body and the head of the code, so follow the instructions carefully. The next step is to add interaction, so we introduce this line of code at the bottom of the piece function:

```
this.pieceButton();
```

Now add these new variables within the `initTriangle` method :

```
this.body.v = 40;                                                    // initial speed
this.body.gravity = 13;                                              // gravity aceleration
this.body.angle = -90+90*(Math.random()-.5);;                        // random initial angle
this.body.vx = this.body.v*Math.cos(this.body.angle*dtr);            // horizontal speed component
this.body.vy = this.body.v*Math.sin(this.body.angle*dtr);            // vertical speed component
this.body.vr = 80*(Math.random()-.5);                                // random rotational speed
```

... and the following methods:

Once the piece is pressed, the `loopJump` method will be triggered:

```
this.piece.prototype.pieceButton = function() {
    this.body.masker.onPress = function() {
      this._parent.ref.loopJump();
    };
};
```

The piece will jump according to parameters angle, v (speed) and gravity. You can see that each piece will describe a parabolic path.

```
this.piece.prototype.loopJump = function() {
    this.body.swapDepths(1000+k++);
    this.body.onEnterFrame = function() {
      this._x += this.vx;
      this._y += this.vy;
      this.vy += this.gravity;
      this._rotation += this.vr;
       if (this._y>=300) {
       this.onEnterFrame = null;
       delete this.ref;
       this.removeMovieClip();
      }
    };
};
```

Once you press the *break* button the image will be broken into many small triangles, and then every time you press a piece, it will jump, disappearing from the stage!

You can modify the code in order to generate different effects. For instance each piece can be moved disappearing to the right side of the stage instead jumping.

mx_explosion_03

We are ready to make our first image explosion – that means that all the pieces will jump at the same moment when we press a "explode" button. To dynamically draw our "explode" button we use the `drawBox` movie clip method

```
createEmptyMovieClip("but", 3);
but.newBox(sx, 350, 90, 20, "explode", 14, 0xffffff, "arial",
➡ "center", 1, 0xffffff, 100, 0x999999, 100);
but._visible = 0;
```

...then we add an event handler, so the box behaves as button. This `onPress` event handler creates a new array. The `st` array holds the objects that have survived the fractal process (remember that every time a triangle is broken, it disappears too).

```
st = [];
this.but02.onPress = function() {
  for (thing in t) {
    t[thing].body._name != null ? st.push(t[thing]) : null;
  }
  for (i=0; i<st.length; i++) {
    st[i].loopJump();
  }
  but02._visible=0;
};
```

Finally, change this line of code within the constructor function. This way the explode button will be visible once the fractal process has finished.

```
this.body.level<maxlevel ? this.loopFractalTriangle() : but02._visible=1;
```

...and removes the `pieceButton` method and this line of code:

```
this.pieceButton();
```

Press the break button to generate the fractal and then press the "explode" button to destroy the image. It's fun.

Remember that this process is very CPU intensive so my advice is don't use more than 3 fractal levels or your system may crash!

mx_explosion_04

Now we want to make it so that once the "explode" button is pressed, all the pieces start jumping one-by-one. Once the `st` array has been filled, it can be sorted using the following functions. :

```
function order(a, b) {
  return a.body._y<b.body._y ? -1 : a.body._y>b.body._y ? 1 : 0;
}

function disorder() {
  return Math.round(Math.random());
}
```

At this stage, we press the button and the jump process begins:

```
st = [];
this.but02.onPress = function() {
  but02._visible = 0;
  for (thing in t) {
    t[thing].body._name != undefined ? st.push(t[thing]) : null;
  }
  st.sort(order);
  index=0, frame=0;
  this.onEnterFrame = function() {
    frame==0 ? st[index].loopJump() : null;
```

```
        frame++;
        if (frame>=3) {
            index++;
            frame = 0;
        }
        index>=st.length ? this.onEnterFrame=null : null;
    };
};
```

We have included an `onEnterFrame` event handler to add some delay between every jump.

nx_explosion_05

We are ready to code our slide show. The first step is to generate an array of images for our slide show (keep in mind that you must set up the library linkage of every image).

```
maxlevel = 2;
dtr = Math.PI/180;
sx=Stage.width/2, sy=Stage.height/2;
images = 2;
image = 0;
imageArray = ["image01", "image02", "image03"]; //the array of images
this.createEmptyMovieClip("img", 1);
img.attachMovie(imageArray[image], "image", 1);
iw=img._width/2, ih=img._height/2;
img._x=sx, img._y=sy;
createEmptyMovieClip("but01", 2);                    // "break" button
but01.newBox(sx, sy+ih+30, 90, 20, "broke", 14, 0xffffff,
➥ "arial", "center", 1, 0xffffff, 100, 0x999999, 100);
createEmptyMovieClip("but02", 3);                    // "explode" button
but02.newBox(sx, sy+ih+30, 90, 20, "explode", 14,
➥ 0xffffff, "arial", "center", 1, 0xffffff, 100, 0x999999, 100);
but02._visible = 0;
function reset() {
    but01._visible = 0;
    img._visible = 0;
    angle = 360*Math.random();
    r = 20+30*Math.random();
    angle = 360*Math.random();
    rx = r*Math.cos(angle*dtr);
    ry = r*Math.sin(angle*dtr);
    x0=sx+rx, y0=sy+ry;
    t = [];
    st = [];
    t[kk++] = new piece(sx-iw, sy+ih, x0, y0, sx-iw, sy-ih, 1);
    t[kk++] = new piece(sx-iw, sy-ih, x0, y0, sx+iw, sy-ih, 1);
    t[kk++] = new piece(sx+iw, sy-ih, x0, y0, sx+iw, sy+ih, 1);
    t[kk++] = new piece(sx+iw, sy+ih, x0, y0, sx-iw, sy+ih, 1);
}
this.but01.onPress = function() {
    reset();
};

this.but02.onPress = function() {
    img._visible = 1;
```

```
    };
  };
```

We have added a `reset` function that will be called every time we break a new image.

Every time the "explode" button is pressed, we attach a new image, and when the last piece of the broken image has jumped the "break" button appears, so the process begins again.

Finally, change this line of code within the `init` method:

```
  this.body.masked.attachMovie(imageArray[image], "img", 1);
```

mx_explosion_06sq

As a last experiment, I want to show you the automatic version of our slide show. I have also included another kind of shape. This time we are going to use rectangles instead triangles. The explosion process can be visualized in the following sequence of images.

This is the new `piece` constructor function

```
  function piece(x1, y1, x2, y2, x3, y3, x4, y4, level) {
    this.initRectangle(x1, y1, x2, y2, x3, y3, x4, y4, level);
    this.drawRectangle();
    if (this.body.level<maxlevel) {
      this.loopFractalRectangle();
    } else {
      if (flag == 0) {
        flag = 1;
        pause(jump, jumpdelay);
      }
    }
  }
```

have also modified the methods because the rectangle shape has got 4 vertices. The new baricenter is the point (x5,y5).

```
this.piece.prototype.initRectangle = function(x1, y1, x2, y2, x3, y3, x4, y4, level) {
  this.body = createEmptyMovieClip("bodyholder"+k, 1000+k++);
  this.body.level = level;
  this.body.ref = this;
  this.body.x1=x1, this.body.x2=x2, this.body.x3=x3, this.body.x4=x4,
  ➥ this.body.x5=x1+(3+4*Math.random())/10*(x4-x1);
  this.body.y1=y1, this.body.y2=y2, this.body.y3=y3, this.body.y4=y4,
  ➥ this.body.y5=y2+(3+4*Math.random())/10*(y4-y2);
  this.body.masked = this.body.createEmptyMovieClip("masked", 1);
  this.body.masker = this.body.createEmptyMovieClip("masker", 2);
  this.body.masked.attachMovie(imageArray[image], "img", 1);
  this.body.masked._x = sx-this.body.x5;
  this.body.masked._y = sy-this.body.y5;
  this.body.masked.setMask(this.body.masker);
  this.mycolor = new Color(this.body);
  this.ran = -100+200*Math.random();
  this.mycolor.setTransform({ra:100, rb:this.ran, ga:100, gb:this.ran, ba:100, bb:this.ran, aa:100, ab:0});
  this.body._x = this.body.x5;
  this.body._y = this.body.y5;
  this.body.v = 40;
  this.body.gravity = 13;
  this.body.angle = -90+90*(Math.random()-.5);
  this.body.vx = this.body.v*Math.cos(this.body.angle*dtr);
  this.body.vy = this.body.v*Math.sin(this.body.angle*dtr);
  this.body.vr = 80*(Math.random()-.5);
};

this.piece.prototype.loopJump = function() {
  this.body.swapDepths(1000+k++);
```

```
      this.ref.mycolor.setTransform({ra:100, rb:this.ref.ran, ga:100, gb:this.ref.ran, ba:100,
      ➥ bb:this.ref.ran, aa:100, ab:0});
      break;
    case 3 :
      t[kk++] = new piece(this.x1, this.y1, this.x1, this.y5, this.x5, this.y5, this.x5, this.y1, this.level+1);
      break;
    case 5 :
      t[kk++] = new piece(this.x1, this.y5, this.x2, this.y2, this.x5, this.y2, this.x5, this.y5, this.level+1);
      break;
    case 7 :
      t[kk++] = new piece(this.x5, this.y5, this.x5, this.y2, this.x3, this.y3, this.x3, this.y5, this.level+1);
      break;
    case 9 :
      t[kk++] = new piece(this.x5, this.y4, this.x5, this.y5, this.x3, this.y5, this.x4, this.y4, this.level+1);
      break;
    case 10 :
      delete this.ref;
      this.removeMovieClip();
      break;
    }
    counter++;
  };
};

this.piece.prototype.drawRectangle = function() {
  this.body.masker.beginFill(0x000000, 100);
  this.body.masker.lineStyle(0, 0xffffff, 100);
  this.body.masker.moveTo(this.body.x1-this.body.x5, this.body.y1-this.body.y5);
  this.body.masker.lineTo(this.body.x2-this.body.x5, this.body.y2-this.body.y5);
  this.body.masker.lineTo(this.body.x3-this.body.x5, this.body.y3-this.body.y5);
  this.body.masker.lineTo(this.body.x4-this.body.x5, this.body.y4-this.body.y5);
  this.body.masker.lineTo(this.body.x1-this.body.x5, this.body.y1-this.body.y5);
  this.body.masker.endFill();
};

function order(a, b) {
  return a.body._y<b.body._y ? -1 : a.body._y>b.body._y ? 1 : 0;
}
```

We include a pause function, that will be called every time we need a time delay. This function receives the name of the delayed function and the delay (number of frames) as parameters.

```
function pause(myfunction, mydelay) {
  var frame = 0, pausedfunction = myfunction;
  this.onEnterFrame = function(myfunction) {
    if (frame++ == mydelay) {
      this.onEnterFrame = null;
      pausedfunction();
    }
  };
}
```

We don't need buttons, so remove the "break" and "explode" buttons; we have 2 functions (`reset` and `jump`) that perform the animation.

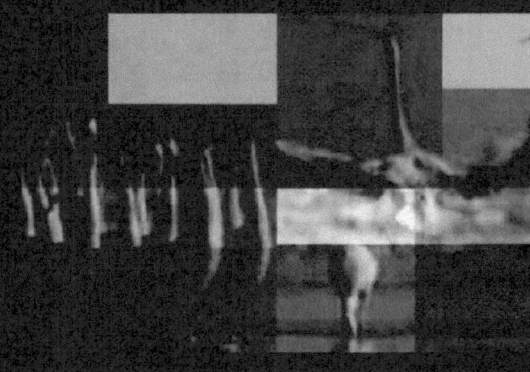

```
maxlevel =3;
dtr = Math.PI/180;
sx=Stage.width/2, sy=Stage.height/2;
images = 2;
image = 0;
imageArray = ["image01", "image02", "image03"];
this.createEmptyMovieClip("img", 1);
img.attachMovie(imageArray[image], "image", 1);
iw=img._width/2, ih=img._height/2;
img._x=sx, img._y=sy;
jumpdelay = 30;
breakdelay = 50;
function reset() {
    flag = 0;
    t = [];
    st = [];
    var x1 = sx-iw, y1 = sy+ih;
    var x2 = sx-iw, y2 = sy-ih;
    var x3 = sx+iw, y3 = sy-ih;
    var x4 = sx+iw, y4 = sy+ih;
    t[kk++] = new piece(x1, y1, x2, y2, x3, y3, x4, y4, 1);
}
function jump() {
    image<images ? image++ : image=0;
    img.attachMovie(imageArray[image], "image", 1);
    for (thing in t) {
      t[thing] body._name != undefined ? st.push(t[thing]) : null;
    }
    st.sort(order);
    var index = 0, frame = 0;
    _root.onEnterFrame = function() {
      frame == 0 ? st[index].loopJump() : null;
      frame++;
      if (frame>=3) {
        index++;
        frame = 0;
      }
      if (index == st.length) {
        this.onEnterFrame = null;
        pause(reset, breakdelay);
      }
    };
}
pause(reset, 50);
stop();
```

Done!. We have finished our advanced image slide show and the explosion effect using the new dynamic masking and drawing API functions. You can improve this application using external images (remember that you will need an image preloader in order to check if the image has been loaded).

I hope you've enjoyed our experiments with masks and masking. Mess with the code, the variables, and change the JPGs.. Remember, you can't break anything, and even if your SWFs crash and burn they might give you just the inspiration you've been looking for.

experimental interfaces
paul prudence

The movie clip object is at the core of Flash. ActionScript control of the movie clip has always been at the center of any great Flash work with its numerous methods and properties. Now in Flash MX it has been given a fabulous new set of methods, properties, and most importantly, event handlers to give us much greater control, more precision and greater versatility in the scripting environment. Exciting new features in MX include the ability to create new movie clips on the fly at runtime. The new drawing API allows us to dynamically populate such movie clips with lines, curves, fills and gradients on the fly as the movie is playing. A particularly brilliant new addition to the ActionScript lexicon is the ability to ascribe events to movie clips much in the same way you would give buttons event handlers. What's more, the old methodology of attaching code to movie clips and buttons has given way to a much more structured and centralized method akin to real OOP languages. It's now possible for all of your code to reside in one place. Other exciting advances include the ability to dynamically load external media such as JPGs and MP3s, I could go on but I would like to give each of these more time and look at them in more detail as I work through a set of creative experimental interfaces with variations utilizing many of these new features and more.

Advances in the MX scripting environment lend themselves amazingly well to interface design where quite often we have a situation where lots of buttons have similar traits and properties but remain unique in some functionality. For a non-programmer artist/designer like myself this is a breath of fresh air since I can concentrate on aesthetics without getting too lost in a pile of hermetic hitTest array loop checks! Put simply it's just a lot easier to accomplish certain tasks in MX – in Flash 5 the limitations of the scripting model meant often resorting to programming workarounds. Throughout this chapter I'll be offering explanations of how my code might have fared in Flash 5 and how in many cases the tasks in hand would have been impossible.

Experimental interface and the working process

The interface experiments I'm going to work through have been arrived at from an exploration of the use of multiple units arranged in non-ordinary interface configurations, geometric forms outside of the standard rectilinear formation (namely rows of buttons. I wanted an interface that had some discrete and unique beauty of its own apart from, and outside of, the site's content. As long as usability remained a key attribute and there was some sequential method for interaction I wanted an interface that you might want to play with for a little while, not something entirely functional to the point that it was only there to be clicked to get to something else. Running the risk of offending the usability police, I wanted something that on first encounter the user couldn't be quite 100% sure of.

The vast majority of my time in Flash is spent in explorative mode, making things, breaking things, adding new variables to the system, adding a new trig function here or there – quite often with no purpose in mind – it's a lot like playing with Meccano. Every now and then something happens, an interesting effect is produced and the start of a small adventure is embarked upon. I used to do a lot of painting and the same process occurs there, a form of alchemy when things start to flow and you say a-ha!

The files in this chapter are, I believe, at that point, at the end of the experimentation process and the start of the refinement process. It's interesting to note that quite often near the end of a refinement process I'll take a finished piece and start to break it again – adding antagonistic code to make something new. So this whole process of experimentation and refinement is cyclic and intermingled – experimentation is always at the heart of it somewhere, it's the food of the process.

As we shall see, Flash MX lends itself remarkably well to experimentation due to its improved internal code structure, it's now just a lot easier to hybridize our code, but more on that as we go on.

I'm going to work through two interfaces, each with a number of developed variations resulting from changes to the core code. I'll be looking at the core code in detail, with the variations I'll take a close look at the specific modifications. Finally I'll be offering possible routes to continue with in our experiments, so here we go.

Experiment 1 – An experimental drawing API interface created at runtime

Have a look at the code below all contained in frame one of the movie `API_circles01.fla`. You can download this, and all the other files for this chapter from www.friendsofED.com. Open it up, test it in your browser - then we'll delve into how it's created.

`API_circles01.fla`

```
// the links
// ———
var link = ["circle09", "circle08", "circle07", "circle06", "circle05", "circle04", "circle03",
➡"circle02", "circle01", "circle09", "circle08", "circle07", "circle06", "circle05", "circle04",
➡"circle03", "circle02", "circle01", "circle09", "circle08", "circle07", "circle06", "circle05",
➡"circle04", "circle03", "circle02", "circle01", "circle09", "circle08", "circle07", "circle06",
➡"circle05", "circle04", "circle03", "circle02", "circle01", "circle09", "circle08", "circle07",
➡"circle06", "circle05", "circle04", "circle03", "circle02", "circle01", "circle09", "circle08",
➡"circle07", "circle06", "circle05", "circle04", "circle03", "circle02", "circle01"];

//draw circle proto
//————-
MovieClip.prototype.drawCircle = function(xpos, ypos, radius, lWidth, lColor,
➡fColor,fAlpha) {
    x = xpos;
    y = ypos;
    r = radius;
    u = r*0.4086;
    v = r*0.7071;
    this.lineStyle(lwidth,lColor,100);
    this.beginFill(fColor, fAlpha);
    this.moveTo(x-r, y);
    this.curveTo(x-r, y-u, x-v, y-v);
    this.curveTo(x-u, y-r, x, y-r);
    this.curveTo(x+u, y-r, x+v, y-v);
    this.curveTo(x+r, y-u, x+r, y);
    this.curveTo(x+r, y+u, x+v, y+v);
    this.curveTo(x+u, y+r, x, y+r);
    this.curveTo(x-u, y+r, x-v, y+v);
    this.curveTo(x-r, y+u, x-r, y);
    this.endFill();
};
```

```
// create circles and add events
// ———————
for (i = 0; i < link.length; i++) {
    _root.createEmptyMovieClip("mc'+i, i);
    with ( _root["mc'+i] ) {
        drawCircle(0,0,20,1,0xFFffff,0xFD0E02*i/1,25);
        drawCircle(0,0,5,1,0xFFffff,0xFD0E02*i/1,25);
        _x = Math.sin (i)*(50-Math.sqrt(i)*15)+Math.sin(i)+250;
        _y = Math.cos (i)*(50-Math.sqrt(i)*55)+Math.cos(i)+250;
    }

    // the rollOver
    // ———
    _root["mc"+i].onRollOver = function(){
        _root.createEmptyMovieClip("rol", 1000);
        rol.drawCircle(this._x,this._y,30,1,0xAFA374,0xffffff,40);
        this._yscale = this._xscale = 110;
        _root.createEmptyMovieClip("line", 1005);
        with ( _root.line ) {
            lineStyle( 1, 0xAFA374, 50 );
            moveTo( this._x, this._y  );
            lineTo(386,191);
        }
        _root.select = " " + _root.link[Number((this._name).substring(2)]]
    }

    // the rollOut
    // ———
    _root["mc"+i].onRollOut = function(){
        rol.clear();
        this._yscale = this._xscale = 100
    }

    // the release - load relative jpg
    // ———————
    _root["mc"+i].onRelease = function(){
        _root.createEmptyMovieClip("line2", 1006);
        with ( _root.line2 ) {
            lineStyle( 1, 0xAFA374, 75 );
            moveTo( this._x, this._y  );
            lineTo(386,191);
        }
        toload = select + ".jpg";
        _root.createEmptyMovieClip("jpg_parent",-1);
        with ( _root.jpg_parent ) {
            _x = 384;
            _y = 106;
            loadMovie(toload, 0);
        }
    }
}
```

circle06

```
// the label
// ———-
_root.createEmptyMovieClip("label", 1002);
_root.label.createTextField("insidelabel",1003,100,-20,50,18);
_root.label.insidelabel.background = true;
_root.label.onEnterFrame = function () {
    yslide = (_root._ymouse - this._y) * .2;
    this._y += yslide;
    _root.label.insidelabel.text = _root.select;
}
```

circle02

Look at the ActionScript in Flash MX. Notice that there is nothing in the library, no symbols at all! Everything needed to generate the interface is contained within the single first frame of the movie – cool huh? When the movie is fired up this code does everything from drawing the circular buttons to attaching the event handlers (rollovers and press functions) to opening the desired files when the buttons are pressed. This is something that could never have been done in Flash 5 as the circular buttons would have to have been drawn manually and then added to the library from where they could have been referenced by a script often using the attachMovie method.

The movie clip object in Flash MX now has an exciting array of drawing methods that allow us to instruct Flash to draw lines, curves and fills and by extension any complex shape you care to imagine. This is all very well but what if we want to control these new shapes? Well we can, thanks to a new ability in MX to create empty movieclips as holders for anything we care to put inside them. Since an interface relies on user interaction to work there is one other great addition to the movie clip object in MX we can utilize and that is the ability to add an event chain to them and make them behave just like buttons. This may not seem so great at first glance since we already have buttons, and they too have had a wonderful overhaul in MX, but as we shall see, the implications are tremendous in more ways than one.

Enough talk, let's dip into the code a block at a time.

Picture this

First off I'm defining an array list of all JPGs that I want to load via my interface. This array could contain any number of items, the final number of buttons on the screen will be dependent on the amount of items in array, I've re-used the same JPGs a number of times, but it would be possible to have, say, 60 entirely different circles...

```
var link = ["circle60", "circle59", ... , "circle02", "circle01"]
```

The JPGs themselves need to be in the same directory as the published SWF – if you don't add the absolute URL or folder location of the images.

Draw!

Next I'm going to use the new MX API drawing methods to make a movie clip prototype called 'drawCircle'. This prototype function takes a number of arguments that allow us to use `drawCircle` as a movie clip method to make circles with specific properties such as radius, position and fill color. The drawing API is one of the most exciting new features in MX and in many cases will allow us to replace what would have been many lines of code in Flash 5 to just few in MX. The basic commands allow us to define line styles, i.e. line color, line thickness and line opacity (_alpha). We can draw lines and curves from point to point, and with the shapes made we can apply solid or gradient fills. We also have the option to pick up the pen and move it to another position on the screen without making a mark.

The circle code I've used is a little more complicated than we might expect. Surely we can make a circle using four curves at 90 degrees to one another? Well we can but MX has a habit of making non-perfect circles with this method, in fact they appear somewhat square, and a square circle is too non-conformist, even for me! MX fails on the accuracy front regarding curves of that angular size, however with a little bit of math and eight 45 degree angled curves we can achieve a perfect circle with ease!

```
//draw circle proto
//———————-
MovieClip.prototype.drawCircle =
➡function(xpos, ypos, radius, lWidth,
➡lColor, fColor, fAlpha) {
    x = xpos;
    y = ypos;
    r = radius;
    u = r*0.4086;
    v =  r*0.7071;
    this.lineStyle(lwidth,lColor,100);
    this.beginFill(fColor, fAlpha);
    this.moveTo(x-r, y);
    this.curveTo(x-r, y-u, x-v, y-v);
    this.curveTo(x-u, y-r, x, y-r);
    this.curveTo(x+u, y-r, x+v, y-v);
    this.curveTo(x+r, y-u, x+r, y);
    this.curveTo(x+r, y+u, x+v, y+v);
    this.curveTo(x+u, y+r, x, y+r);
    this.curveTo(x-u, y+r, x-v, y+v);
    this.curveTo(x-r, y+u, x-r, y);
    this.endFill();
}
```

The possibilities for use of the drawing API in MX are virtually limitless. We can expect to see the hardcore few experimenting at the fringes of math and creativity producing some stunning work. More so, a great deal of files, like this one, will be published without a single movie clip or symbol in the library! A lot of 3D work in previous versions of Flash was hampered by processor unfriendly routines that worked hard just drawing these objects to be manipulated in 3D space. The ability to draw lines to points will really push such work to a new level and allow developers to concentrate solely on the 3D engines.

Next we are going to set a `for` loop to loop as many times as there are items in the array we have just defined. Length is a property of an array returning the number of items in the array, so in this case the loop will loop 60 times. The next line utilizes a new feature in MX, the ability to create an empty movie clip. Anyone familiar with Flash 5's `attachMovie` will be instantly at home as it has a very similar syntax requiring an instance name and a depth. The next line of code specifies a set of properties/methods for the `"mc"+i` instance within the curly braces using the `with` statement. This prevents you from having to repeatedly write the object's name or the path to the object. The first two lines within the `with` statement call upon the previously defined `drawCircle` function to make two circles in that particular instance of the newly created movie clip. The arguments passed to the `drawCircle` function that define these two circles are as follows in this order: x-position, y-position, radius, line width, line color, fill color and fill alpha. We can see for example that both circles are positioned top left within the new movie clip and the second circle is a quarter of the size of the first. We can further see that the colors of these circles will be different as they are dependent upon the value of i. Because the alpha is set to 25% for both, the result is a collection of hues pleasing to my eyes. The final two lines of code in this block set the x and y positions of each respective movie clip based on some math functions. I experiment quite a bit with plotting movieclips according to these kinds of functions, quite often I find unique shapes and geometric formations lying hidden and revealed by code tweaks and experimentation. I will come back to alter these lines quite a bit in later mutations of this file.

```
// Create circles and add events
// —————————
for (i = 0; i < link.length; i++) {
    _root.createEmptyMovieClip("mc"+i, i);
    with ( _root["mc"+i] ) {
        drawCircle(0, 0, 20, 1, 0xFFffff,
        ➡0xFD0E02*i/1, 25)
        drawCircle(0, 0, 5, 1, 0xFFffff,
        ➡0xFD0E02*i/1, 25)
        _x = Math.sin(i)*(50-Math.sqrt(i)
        ➡*15) + Math.sin(i)+250;
        _y = Math.cos (i)*(50-Math.sqrt(i)
        ➡*55) + Math.cos(i)+250;
    }
}
```

▶lay

he next step is to give our circles some interactivity and
his is where one of the best new features in MX comes into
▶lay – and that is the ability to add button functionality to
he humble movie clip object by virtue of a new set of event
andlers. Not only can we add the kind of functionality
▶reviously only reserved for buttons but we don't even have
o attach them to our movieclips as we did with our
▶uttons. We can define event callback functions and attach
hem remotely to the movieclips via a centralized piece of
ode in this case in the first frame of our movie.

et's digress from the circles code for a moment and take
▶n example of how things have changed. In Flash 5 the
▶yntax for adding *events* to buttons would have been
▶omething like this:

```
on ( release ) {
    perform the task
}
```

▶n MX we can do this – placing the code in the main
▶imeline:

```
theMC.onRelease = function () {
    perform the task
}
```

▶his syntactical structure is much more in keeping with real
▶OP languages, in fact it is a subset of OOP rather like
▶avaScript. It has distinct advantages over the old Flash 5 way
▶f doing things.

OK, now returning to our circles example, let's look at our
code for the rollover state of one of our clip instances. We
are still in the for loop and this allows us to attach an event
to every single instance i.e. "mc"+i. The first line in our
event function creates a new movie clip called rol with a
depth of 1000. I've chosen a depth of 1000 so we can be
sure it exists high enough in the stack never to be interfered
with by other movie clip instances. The next line instructs
Flash to draw a circle at the position of the mouse cursor, as
this is directly over one of our "mc"+i clip instances it
positions the circle exactly over the movie clip we are rolling
over and in our movie actually gives a nice snap-to rollover
effect. Following this we have set the scaling of our
particular mc to 110% adding to the rollover effect. For
schematic clarity in this interface I wanted to show a line
connecting our rolled over mc to our loading area where
our JPGs appear so again we create an empty movie clip and
populate it with a line. An 0xAFA374 colored line 1 pixel
wide with 50% alpha connects the registration point of our
movie clip, which, by default conveniently for us, is the
center of our specific mc, to position 386,191 on the stage –
and this links to a circle containing the loaded content.
Finally in this block of code, the _root variable select is
set to a value in the link array dependent on the movie
clip's instance name. This is a great way of individually iden-
tifying a particular movie clip amongst many that have been
generated on the fly. What we have done is to convert the
third character and onwards in the instance name string of
the particular movie clip into a number which is useful for
referring to that array. We have also added a character
space at the start of this string for design purposes.

```
// the rollOver
// ———
_root["mc"+i].onRollOver = function(){
    _root.createEmptyMovieClip("rol",1000);
    rol.drawCircle(this._x, this._y, 30, 1,
    ➡0xAFA374, 0xffffff, 40);
    this._yscale = this._xscale = 110;
    _root.createEmptyMovieClip("line",1005);
    with ( _root.line ) {
        lineStyle( 1, 0xAFA374, 50 );
        moveTo( this._x, this._y );
        lineTo(386,191);
    }
    _root.select = " " + _root.link[Number
    ➡((this._name).substring(2))];
}
```

Now we will look at the rollout event. Using the clear method, which is also new to MX, we remove all the drawing commands associated the rol movie clip. This is essence makes the large white rollover circle disappear. We also want the individual mc to return to its original scale so we set the x and y scale back to 100%.

```
// the rollOut
// ———
_root["mc"+i].onRollOut = function(){
    rol.clear();
    this._yscale = this._xscale = 100;
}
```

Next up are the events ascribed to clicking on one of our circles, the onRelease event. When the movie clip is released we have again created an empty movie clip called line2 at a free depth. Just like we did with the rollover function we draw a line from the center of the movie clip to 384,106 on the stage, this time with greater weight. We can see from the fact that these line clips are drawn freshly each time the onRelease is triggered that they will erase the previous versions of the drawn line. You can see in the final SWF that the combinations of movieclips line1 and line2 give a schematic representation of the circles to be clicked and the circles currently clicked.

The next three lines of code are the ones that load the JPG into the SWF. Previously in Flash the only external media we could load into SWFs were other SWFs. MX has now given us the wonderful ability to load both external JPGs and MP3s on the fly. This is great addition to MX because it means no more having to load all JPGs contained within a SWF before the file gets going. We can now load each JPG when a user requires it cutting down on preloading time dramatically, this will be of particular benefit to Flash photography portfolios for example. Going back to the code, first up we set the variable toload to add together the string variable select and the string ".jpg". Next we create an empty movie clip holder called 'jpg_parent' at a depth of -1 and position it in the correct spot on the stage ready for the final bit of code which is loadMovie(toload, 0). Remember toload will be equal to circle(x).jpg where x is a number between 1 and 60. That's all the code for movie clip interaction.

```
// the release + load relative jpg
// ———————————
_root["mc"+i].onRelease = function(){
    _root.createEmptyMovieClip("line2", 1006);
    with ( _root.line2 ) {
        lineStyle( 1, 0xAFA374, 75 );
        moveTo( this._x, this._y );
        lineto(386,191);
    }
    toload = select + ".jpg";
    _root.createEmptyMovieClip("jpg_parent",-1);
    with ( _root.jpg_parent ) {
        _x = 384;
        _y = 106;
        loadMovie(toload, 0);
    }
}
```

The last block of code is used to generate a label showing us the name of the item we are rolling over. Again we are going to generate this on the fly using the new MX `createTextField` method which creates a text field object inside of another newly created empty movie clip called 'label'. You can now see how indispensable the MX `createEmptyMovieclip` method is since we have used it a lot throughout this script and couldn't have got by without it.

Going back to the `createTextField` method we can see that it takes a number of arguments and in order they are: instanceName, depth, x, y, width, and height. Once created, the text field has a number of default properties that can be set that are both stylistic and of a functional nature, for example you can set the text to appear in password star form or add a border to the field. Here I've turned on the background, I can then go on to specify a color if I want but the default white is fine for now. Any text field created in this manner also gets its own default `TextFormat` object which defines the text formatting of the text field, for example font type, size, alignment etc. We'll look at this later in the second experiment. To give the label a bit of life I've added a sliding inertia `onEnterFrame` function so that the label glides towards the mouse   pointer on the y axis. Last of all we need to populate the text field with the current movie clip name while rolling over it so we must set text to the value of `_root.select`, this is reset every frame so that text is kept up to date with whatever movie clip we are currently rolling over.

```
// the label
// ——-
_root.createEmptyMovieClip("label", 1002);
_root.label.createTextField("insidelabel",1003,100,-20,50,18);
_root.label.insidelabel.background = true;
_root.label.onEnterFrame = function () {
    yslide = (_root._ymouse - this._y) * .2;
    this._y += yslide;
    _root.label.insidelabel.text = _root.select;
}
```

That's it! A complete Flash MX interface generated at runtime weighing in at 1.33 Kilobytes and occupying one frame on the timeline! Not bad. The code is all in one place which means that on going back to this file everything will be easy to find, update and change. If I want to grab a portion of code and take it to another file I don't have to worry about importing the movie clip the code is attached to because it not attached to anything, this makes for great modular coding. I quite like this interface, its simplicity and tonal variation work – however Flash is all about motion, so let's develop this core code a bit further with a few tweaks and additions and give it some movement. Quite often the smallest of changes yield the greatest result, let's also make a few changes to the positioning of the movieclips.

API DNA

Some changes to the core code and we have an animated nucleic structured menu. The circle buttons are arranged in a spiraling chain and can be revolved in either direction with the mouse pointer, quite a large jump from the initial interface! Let's have a summary of the changes.

Open up `API_nucleic.fla` and look at the script. In the first part of our loop we can see that the two lines defining the size and color of our circles have been modified. The x and y positions of our newly made circles inside each movie clip are now dependent on some trigonometric functions of i, and this is what gives the final form a DNA look. The radii and colors have been changed as well as the x and y plotting positions.

```
drawCircle(Math.sin(i)*10,Math.cos(i)*20,17,1,0xFFffff,0xFD0E02*i/1,15);
drawCircle(Math.sin(i)*10,Math.cos(i)*20,10,1,0xFFffff,0xFD0E02*i/8.5,45);
_x = 275;
_y = 35+(i*16);
```

Regarding the rollout, rollover and release events – I've mainly taken code out. The lines pointing to the JPG load area have gone and the larger white rollover circle has gone. Only the relative scaling of the movie clip's remain. We have added a new event function to the movie clip's and this is:

```
// the enterFrame
// ———
_root["movieclip"+i].onEnterFrame = function(){
    this._rotation-=8*(2-(_root._xmouse/150));
}
```

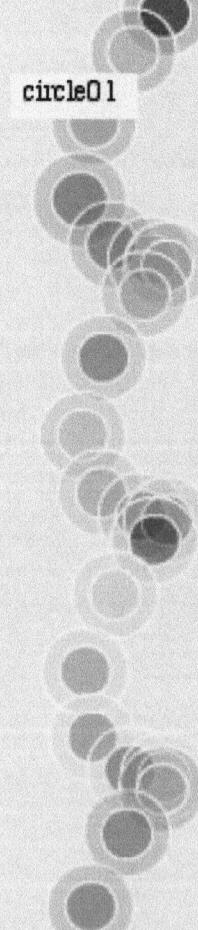

circle01

This piece of code is responsible for creating the twisting motion of the movieclips and is dependent on the relative position of the mouse.

As far as the label goes we've now added a few lines to make the text field slide in the x-axis as well as the y. However when we inadvertently rollover the text field it takes precedence over the circle buttons, and in effect, if the mouse pointer is over both it renders the button out of action. It's OK though, MX has an answer for this in the form of the selectable property of a text field. So we add the following line to our code:

```
_root.label.insidelabel.selectable = false;
```

Your history

I thought it would be interesting to add a history path to this next interface a bit like the one at the excellent uncontrol.com, this gives us a way of seeing the path we've traced as we click on successive items, the final result comes across as linear Hansel (as in Gretel) versus a shifting Venn diagram! Take a look at `API_historyPath.fla` – if you want the full effect you will have to publish and test in your browser. In Flash 5 it was possible to dynamically draw lines from and to specified points but it took a little bit of trickery. In essence you'd use a hairline line contained inside a movie clip and scale it from point to point. With MX using `lineTo` we can perform this task with ease. To draw a line from the last to the next clicked item is a relatively simple task. Included inside the `onRelease` events we've just added and modified a few lines of code. This file takes the last variation as a starting point and adds a few new lines of code. The `onRelease` block now looks like this:

```
// the release - load relative jpg
// ─────────────────
_root["mc"+i].onRelease = function(){
    _root.createEmptyMovieClip("line2", 1005+count);
    with ( _root.line2 ) {
        lineStyle( 1, 0x684522, 10+count);
        moveTo( this._x, this._y );
        lineTo(lastx,lasty );
    }
    lastx = this._x ;
    lasty = this._y;
    count++;
    toload = select + ".jpg";
    _root.createEmptyMovieClip("jpg_parent",2000);
    with ( _root.jpg_parent ) {
        _x = 384;
        _y = 106;
        loadMovie(toload, 0);
    }
}
```

This time when a movie clip is clicked we are creating an empty movie clip at successive levels, this prevents the previous line from being erased when the new one is created. The linestyle's alpha value is set to increment by one each time an movie clip is clicked, this just gives an effect of history since the earlier path lines will be lighter and somewhat further off in distance. The line is drawn to the item we are currently clicking on from the previous item we have just clicked on. The most recently clicked items x and y positions are then set as variables `lastx` and `lasty` ready for the next line to be drawn. The variable `count` is incremented by 1 each time we draw a line, thereby increasing the depth of each newly created movie clip and also making path lines successively darker with each click.

Apart from some color plotting position changes I have also rotated the initial positions of each generated movie clip by a factor of `i*60`.

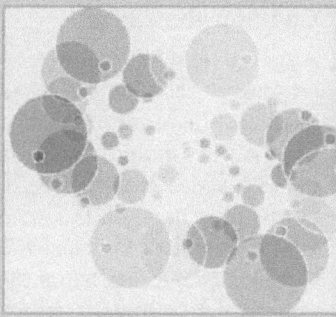
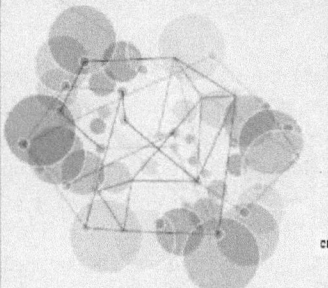
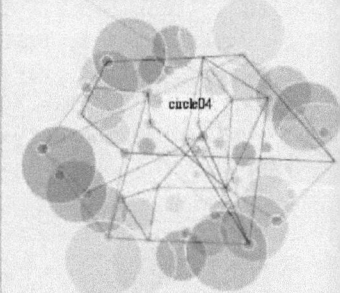
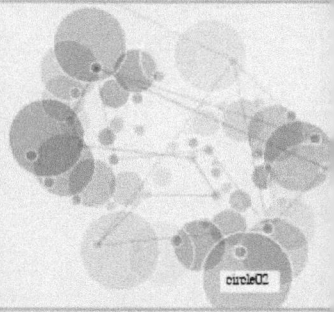
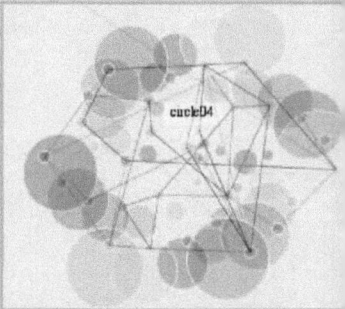

Gnomon the range

A gnomon is a self-repeating shape such as those found in spiral seashells and defined by Fibonacci sequences of numbers. The beautiful forms of the logarithmic (or equi-angular) spirals observed in nature occur when a region of active growth produces inactive material (such as the material of shells and horns) over time. All though our next variation isn't strictly a gnomon it does bare more than a passing resemblance to these kinds of forms, hence the name. Take a look a API_gnomon30.swf, then open up the corresponding API_gnomon30.fla.

Again, taking the last variation as a starting point we've changed the initial properties of the drawn circles, and the plotting positions of the movieclips that contain them. To indicate which item has been clicked this time, I've added a few lines of code that draws a colored line from the movie clip clicked, to the left hand side of the stage, this is contained in the onRelease event function.

```
with ( _root.line2 ) {
    lineStyle( 1, 0xFD0E02/count, 30 );
    moveTo( this._x, this._y );
    lineTo(50, this._y-50 )
    lineTo(0, this._y-50);
}
```

If you experiment with the drawCircle arguments to change the properties of the circles and particularly the three lines of code directly after the drawCircle method you can get quite an amazing range of results.

```
drawCircle(i,0,i/1.5,1,0xffffff,0xFD0E02*i/1,50)
drawCircle(0,i/100,5,1,0xffffff,0xFD0E02*i/1.1,34)
_x = 325;
_y = i*10;
_rotation = i*30
```

The two lines containing the drawCircle movie clip prototype method allow us to define the size, coloring and positioning of the plotted circle buttons. We can, for example dictate the size and color of the circles depending on the sequence of each created button and this makes for some very interesting effects. We can further effect the final positions of the circles with the next two lines, the last line deals with rotational factor of each circle thereby further adding complexity to the plotting positions.

The following sub-variations have had these lines changed in some way or another:
API_gnomon12.swf, API_gnomon30.swf, API_gnomon60.swf API_gnomon120.swf, API_gnomon_tan.swf.

All though the changes were often minimal, the result as seen in these files is quite varied.

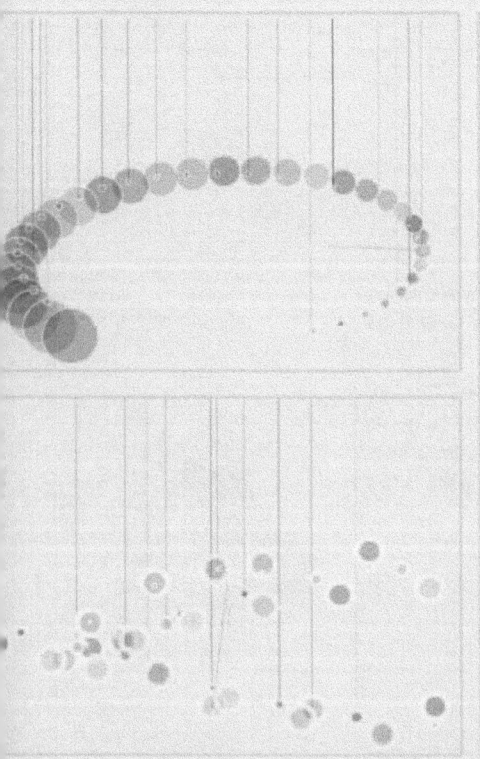
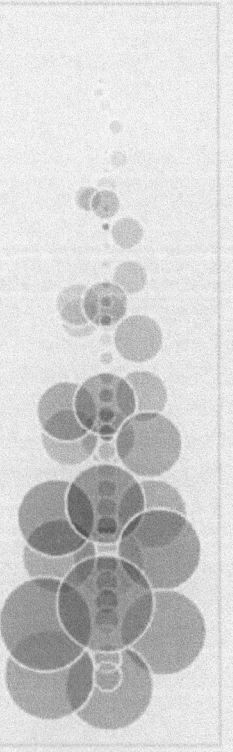
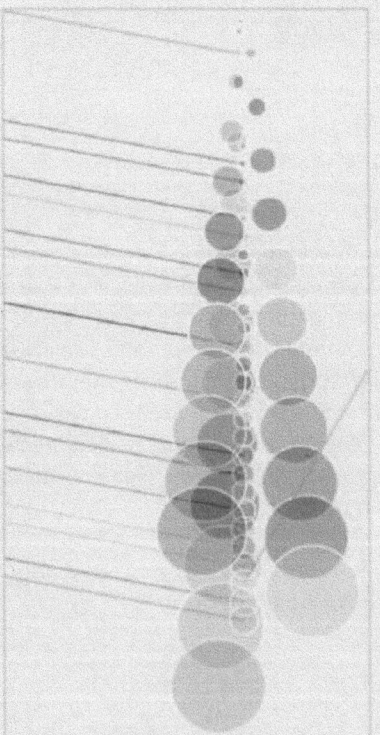
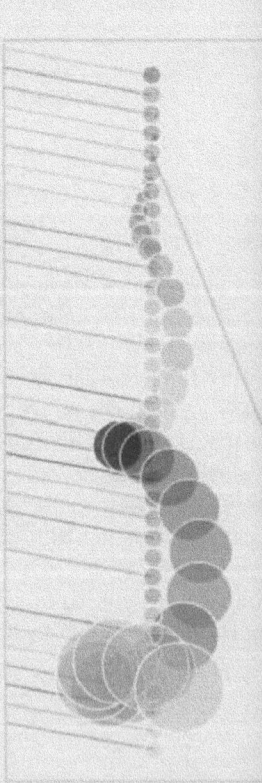

Sway

In the file `API_Undulating.fla` I've made a change to the circle button configurations and re-installed the history path function. The items move with a pleasing undulating effect the nearer the mouse pointer is to the bottom of the stage. This version is almost identical to `API_historyPath.fla` but with a few lines of code modified. The same four lines creating the circles and their respective positions have been changed.

```
drawCircle(0,i/5,2+i/2,1,0xFFffff,0x663300*i/1,25);
drawCircle(0,i/5,5,1,0xFFffff,0xFD0E02*i/1,44);
_x = Math.sin(i*60)*40+300;
_y = i*10;
_rotation = i*30;
```

The important line here is `_x = Math.sin(i*60)*40+300;` as it is what gives the circle buttons the final configuration – two curves intertwining.

The other important change is located in the `onEnterFrame` function, which governs the movement of the circle buttons.

```
_root["mc"+i].onEnterFrame = function(){
    this._rotation+=_root._ymouse/50;
    yslide=(_root._ymouse - this._y) *.1/number((this._name).substring(2));
}
```

The important line here is `this._rotation+=_root._ymouse/50` and this simply rotates each circle button by an amount dependent on _y position of the pointer, essentially giving the final file its undulating appearance.

In the second version (`API_Undulating02.fla` and its respective SWF) the sine function line is altered to become a log based calculation – and as math heads will know, this will change the positioning of our circles.

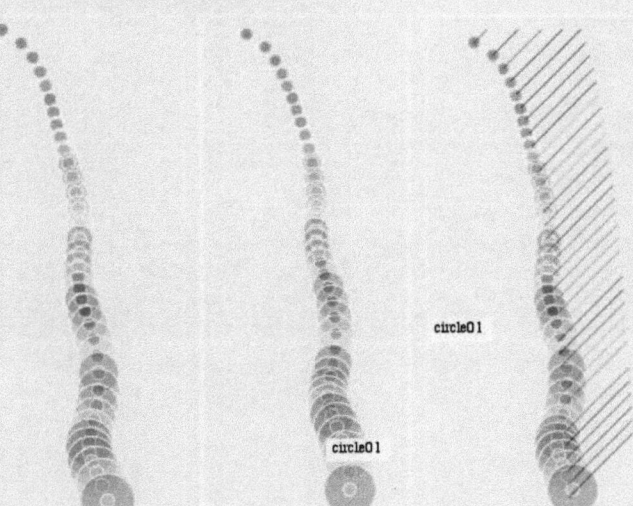

Experiment 2 – An experimental interface using movie clip buttons

This next experiment is closely related to the last in many respects, building up an interface using discrete units as building blocks. However this time instead of having static button objects I want to create a more animated rollover and click effect so I'm going to call to my aid the trusty timeline and do some frame-to-frame tween animation work. As I've mentioned the overhaul of the movie clip in Flash MX is excellent, but as well as movieclips being given new methods and properties the button has now been transformed into a real object with its own methods and properties and you can see that if you create a button and place it on the stage – in the property inspector it has a field to enter an instance name. Once on the stage you can now control with ActionScript its x and y positions, toggle its visibility and all the usual stuff and obviously it still retains all of its event methods, those you used to have to attach to the button in Flash 5. As we have already seen however, the common movie clip now also has these event methods and since you can use it as a button and reference its own timeline, it's actually a lot more powerful at behaving as a button than a button itself!

A button has four frames corresponding to different button states plus one for the hit area. Although we can add animations to these individual frames it can become very messy and often cumbersome, using movieclips as buttons solves this and also give you the possibility of making much more intricate and sophisticated rollover and release effects. Time to run through the file and explain what I mean. First though I must point out that the file uses some nested movieclips and this will help us to understand how the code works. If you have a look at the unit movie clip you will see that contained inside of it is another movie clip called inner and inside of inner is another called inner2.

Here's all of the code which resides in frames 1, 2 and 3:

Frame 1

```
_quality = "LOW";

// pick a rotation constant
// ─────────────
var degrees = [15,30,60,45,90,180,120,10,20];
var rota = degrees[Math.floor(Math.random()*8)];


var link = ["ta-ahet", "ta-khent", "ta-neter", "tchert", "tatau", "tebut",
➡"tem-ra", "tem-kheprer", "tem-thoth", "shepet", "set", "sehkmet",
➡"sheshu-heru", "maat", "annu", "sekhet-bast", "sekhet-nu", "sepes",
➡"nephthys", "net-ra", "amon", "ombos", "heru-em-het", "het-a-khet",
➡"anpu", "apzu", "asar-em-mena", "asar-em-seker", "amtet", "aper-ta"];

//button.Action.function
//─────────────
bAction = function () {
    this.onEnterFrame = function () {
        this.inner._rotation+=2*(2-(_root._xmouse/150));
        this.inner.inner2._rotation-=2*(2-(_root._xmouse/150));
```

```
        if (this.inner.inner2._y < 300 ) {
            this.inner.inner2._y+=13; this.inner._rotation-=2;
        }
    }

    this.onRollOver = function(){
        _root.select = _root.link[number((this._name).substring(4))];
        _root.label._visible = true;
        this.inner.inner2.gotoAndPlay(2);
    }

    this.onRollOut = function (){
        _root.label._visible = false;
        this.inner.inner2.gotoAndPlay(11);
    }

    this.onRelease = function(){
        this.enabled = false ;
        this.inner.inner2.gotoAndPlay(21);
        toload = select + ".jpg";
        _root.createEmptyMovieClip("jpg_parent",2000);
        with ( _root.jpg_parent ) {
            _x = 584;
            _y = 106;
            loadMovie(toload, 0);
        }
    }

}

// the label
// ——
_root.createEmptyMovieClip("label", 1002);
with ( _root.label ) {
    createTextField("insidelabel",1003,20,-20,50,18);
    insidelabel.text = "the label";
    insidelabel.background = true;
    insidelabel.selectable = false;
    insidelabel.autoSize = true;
}
_root.label.onEnterFrame = function () {
    yslide = (_root._ymouse - this._y) * .2;
    this._y += yslide;
    xslide = (_root._xmouse - this._x) * .2;
    this._x += xslide;
    _root.label.insidelabel.text = _root.select;
}
```

heru-em-het

Frame 2

```
// generate button pos. | color code | attach events
// ———————————————————
i++;
attachMovie ("unit", "unit" + i, i);
with (  _root["unit" + i] ) {
    _y = Math.log (i)*(50-Math.sqrt(i)*20)+Math.sin(i)+330;
    _x = Math.log (i)*(50-Math.sqrt(i)*20)+Math.cos(i)+350;
    _rotation = i*rota;
    _yscale = _root["unit" + i]._xscale = 17+(i/4);
    inner.inner2.lineStyle( 60, 0xAFA374*i/9, 20 );
    inner.inner2.moveTo(this._x,this._y);
    inner.inner2.lineto(this._x-1,this._y);
}

bAction.apply(_root["unit" + i]);
if ( i > link.length-2 ) {
    var select="touch.a.sqr"; _root.stop();
}
```

Frame 3

```
gotoAndPlay (2);
```

Now let's run through the codein chunks.

Ra Ra Ra

First up we are going to set the movie quality to low. I've done this for two reasons. The primary reason is that sometimes I think the graphics in Flash look better aliased, and secondly it allows processor unfriendly movies to run real smooth. Next, I define a variable called rota with one of 9 possible values. These nine values have been derived entirely from experimentation and have been found to have useful properties regarding rotation and placement of movieclips. Quite often when you are experimenting you find that certain key variables do unique things to the system, it's good to write them down and use them in a random manner using an array and picking one at random to be used like this. Next up, we have an array defined similarly to the one in the first experiment, so not too much to explain here other than the fact that the names are of Egyptian gods and goddesses, some of them lesser known.

```
_quality = "LOW";

// pick a rotation constant
// ——————————
var degrees = [ 15,30,60,45,90,180,120,10,20];
var rota = degrees[Math.floor(Math.random()*8)];

var link = ["ta-ahet", "ta-khent", "ta-neter", "tchert"];
```

The main event

Have a look at the second block of code starting with the comment `//button.Action.function`. You can see we have defined a number of event functions and they themselves have been encapsulated inside a function called `bAction`. Later we'll attach this whole block of events to our button movieclips. The `onEnterFrame` function takes care of the onscreen animation – notice the use of this is now required whereas in Flash 5 you could omit it as the code would have been attached as an `onClipEvent` function to the actual movieclip – so therefore Flash assumed you were talking to that movieclip's timeline if you left this out. While we're on the subject this illustrates another reason why we should favor movie clip buttons over standard buttons, standard buttons have no timeline to refer to and therefore we cannot refer to them using this.

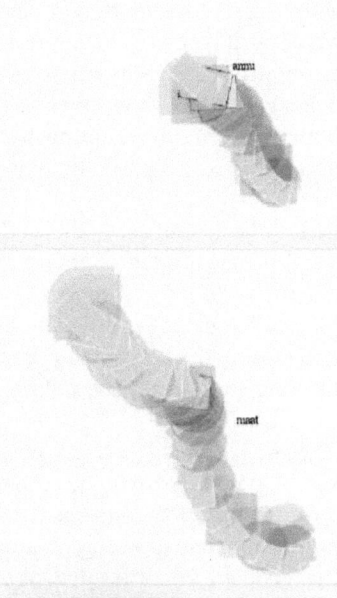

The effect achieved in this file would require quite a bit of trickery if we were to use standard button objects. More to the point, the fact that movieclips can now have event methods solves another problem. we find ourselves up against in previous versions of Flash,. if we were to dynamically generate many buttons on the fly and have events. In Flash 5 if you wanted to give movieclips event functions like rollovers you had to use `hitTest` to test whether the mouse pointer had moved within the boundary of the movieclip. Code would have been attached to each of your movieclip buttons. So whenever the mouse pointer moved over the clip { do something } would have been triggered,. But when you add an `else` statement you start having arguments between each movie clip. For example, if you had attached the script below to all the *movieclips* and you rolled over one of the clips it would try to set x to 1 while all the other clips would be setting it to 0, so you have a conflict.

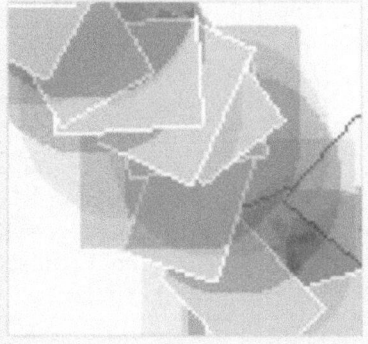

```
onClipEvent (enterFrame) {
    if ( this.hitTest(_root._xmouse, _root._ymouse, true) ) {
        x=1;
    } else {
        x=0;
    }
}
```

Of course, you can get around it by looping through an array of all the clips and checking their states individually, but it's processor unfriendly and messy. MX relieves us of exactly this problem by giving us proper event methods for our movieclips. If you look down at the rollover and rollout states, we set the visibility as on and off for the label clip – much easier!. In Flash 5, we would have to have checked all the movie clip states to perform this task, in MX we only have to look at the one we are interested in.

Inner space

Remember the nested movieclips, `unit` contains `inner` and `inner` contains `inner2` . The first two lines of the `onEnterFrame` function rotates these clips by a certain amount relative to the y co-ordinates of the mouse pointer, what the math actually does is rotate the clips clockwise or anticlockwise depending on how displaced the mouse pointer is from the center, check it out and see.

The next line conditional sets a further rotation and y axis movement dependent on the value of its own inner2's _y value. The onRollOver function determines the value of the variable select in much the same way as previous examples. As we have already mentioned the label is set to _visible. The next line instructs inner2 to play frame 2 of its own timeline. Let's have a look at inner2's timeline.

What I've done basically is to make rollover, rollout and release states that have shape tweens between each state. That way we have an animation for each state – much better than the four frames we get given to play with in a standard button. It allows us the luxury of making very nice animated buttons very easily and without hassle – all we need do is reference the start frame for each state with a gotoAndPlay in each event function as shown below. When we rollover the button the playhead moves to frame 2 and this starts the rollover animation, in this case the movie clip increases in size, changes to white and a plus appears on it. On rollout the button returns to its untouched state. Finally if it is clicked, the playhead moves to frame 21 of inner2's timeline at which point the plus explodes using a shape tween.

One thing to notice in the onRelease function is that fact that button has been set to disabled. This is another new property of movieclips in MX and it comes in handy. Disabling the button at this point is crucial for this movie to work in the way I intend it to. I have an animation tween in the timeline of inner2 and I want it to play right through with the cursor still over the movie clip – without the onRollOver function stepping in and moving the playhead back to a different point in inner2's timeline. If you look at the last frame of inner2's timeline you will see the following code:

```
this._parent._parent.enabled = true ;
```

So after the onRelease part of the animation has been played, the movie clip is brought back to life with button functionality thereby avoiding any timeline conflicts, all thanks to this simple new MX syntax. The rest of the code in this block has already been looked at in the first experiment; it deals with the loading of an external JPG.

```
//button.Action.function
//——————
bAction = function () {

    this.onEnterFrame = function () {
        this.inner._rotation+=2*(2-(_root._xmouse/150));
        this.inner.inner2._rotation-=2*(2-(_root._xmouse/150));
        if (this.inner.inner2._y < 300 ) {
            this.inner.inner2._y+=13; this.inner._rotation-=2
        }
    }

    this.onRollOver = function(){
        _root.select = _root.link[Number((this._name).substring(4))]
        _root.label._visible = true;
        this.inner.inner2.gotoAndPlay(2);
    }

    this.onRollOut = function () {
        _root.label._visible = false;
        this.inner.inner2.gotoAndPlay(11);
    }
```

```
    this.onRelease = function(){
        this.enabled = false ;
        this.inner.inner2.gotoAndPlay(21);
        toload = select + ".jpg";
        _root.createEmptyMovieClip("jpg_parent",2000);
        with ( _root.jpg_parent ) {
            _x = 584;
            _y = 106;
            loadMovie(toload, 0);
        }
    }
}


}
```

he last block of code in frame 1 generates a label like the one in the first experiment. This time we set ome of the text field's properties. The `autoSize` property is set to `true` so that the text field utomatically resizes according to the length of the string inside it – nice and handy. There is a whole senal of text field properties at your disposal. Married up with the `textFormat` object we can expect to e a dizzying array of funky typographical motion experiments in time!

```
// the label
// ———-
_root.createEmptyMovieClip("label", 1002);
with ( _root.label ) {
    createTextField("insidelabel",1003,20,-20,50,18);
    insidelabel.text = "the label";
    insidelabel.background = true;
    insidelabel.selectable = false;
    insidelabel.autoSize = true;
}
_root.label.onEnterFrame = function () {
    yslide = (_root._ymouse - this._y) * .2;
    this._y += yslide;
    xslide = (_root._xmouse - this._x) * .2;
    this._x += xslide;
    _root.label.insidelabel.text = _root.select;
}
```

rame 2

he block of code in the second frame generates the interface button movieclips. This time I've used a ame loop to build up the interface sequentially. Once the loop has 'read' all the items in the array the alue of `touch.a.sqr` is assigned to the variable `select` and the frame loop stops. This time we are lotting button movieclip positions according to log and sin/cos functions of `i` and as you can see in the nal file it gives quite an interesting effect. If you try reloading the file you will see that it builds up a ifferent configuration each time based on those rotational constants we randomly picked earlier – we are otating each successively generated button movieclip by a factor of `i*rota`. The scaling of each is also etermined by a factor of `i`.

Again, I'm going to use the drawing API to color-code each individual movieclip by drawing a very short line but with a large thickness thus making a large circle. I've set the linestyle color to be dependent on the sequence of the movieclips thereby giving some basic form of color coding. If, for example, you replace the line _rotation = i*rota with _rotation = i*180 the code will generate two distinct columns of button movieclips, one column containing red and blue coded buttons and the other green and beige. Its great that you can multiply hexadecimal color values in this way to subtly shift the hues of duplicated clips. You could try changing the divisor of i in the line inner.inner2.lineStyle(60,0xAFA374*i/9,20); to produce different color-coding effects. Lastly, while we are still in the frame loop we'll attach the event functions included in the bAction function to each generated button movieclip using apply.

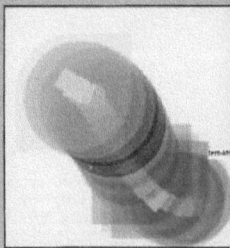

```
// generate button pos. | color code | attach events
// ───────────────────────────
i++;
attachMovie ("unit", "unit" + i, i);
with ( _root["unit" + i] ) {
    _y = Math.log (i)*(50-Math.sqrt(i)*20)+Math.sin(i)+330;
    _x = Math.log (i)*(50-Math.sqrt(i)*20)+Math.cos(i)+350;
    _rotation = i*rota;
    _yscale = _root["unit" + i]._xscale = 17+(i/4);
    inner.inner2.lineStyle( 60, 0xAFA374*i/9, 20 );
    inner.inner2.moveTo(this._x,this._y);
    inner.inner2.lineTo(this._x-1,this._y);
}

bAction.apply(_root["unit" + i]);
if ( i > link.length-2 ) {
    var select="touch.a.sqr" ;
    _root.stop();
}
```

Some of the variations of this file I've produced blur the line between art and interface. In the ubiquitous tug of war between aesthetics and usability, sometimes aesthetics wins out and form dissolves function. To return the desired functionality to a few of these variations we would probably need do some more work in the scripting environment.

Shape changing

Try out the files rota_face_02a.fla to rota_face_02g.fla (or their published SWFs). In variation 2a, I've merely increased the size of the color code circles; the interface is larger and more pronounced. In 2b, I've stretched the color-code circles into tabular shapes and fixed the rotational factor of the generated movieclips to to i*15. In 2c, I've shifted the colors of the tabs and fixed the rotational factor to i*120. I really like the scale of 2d with its large rotating color fields, here I've just upped the scaling and played with the colors again. The rotational movement gets quite complex in variation 2e as the clips spin into and out of particularly defined geometric configurations which I find pleasing to the eye. To achieve this I've modified the respective rotations of the movieclips inner and inner2 inside the onEnterFrame event function in the first frame. Again I've also changed the colors. In variations 2f and 2g I've played with the scaling attributes and the final result I find quite interesting even if the interfaces begins to lose functionality.

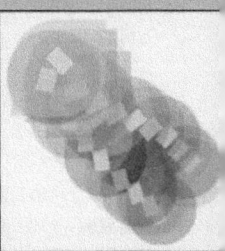

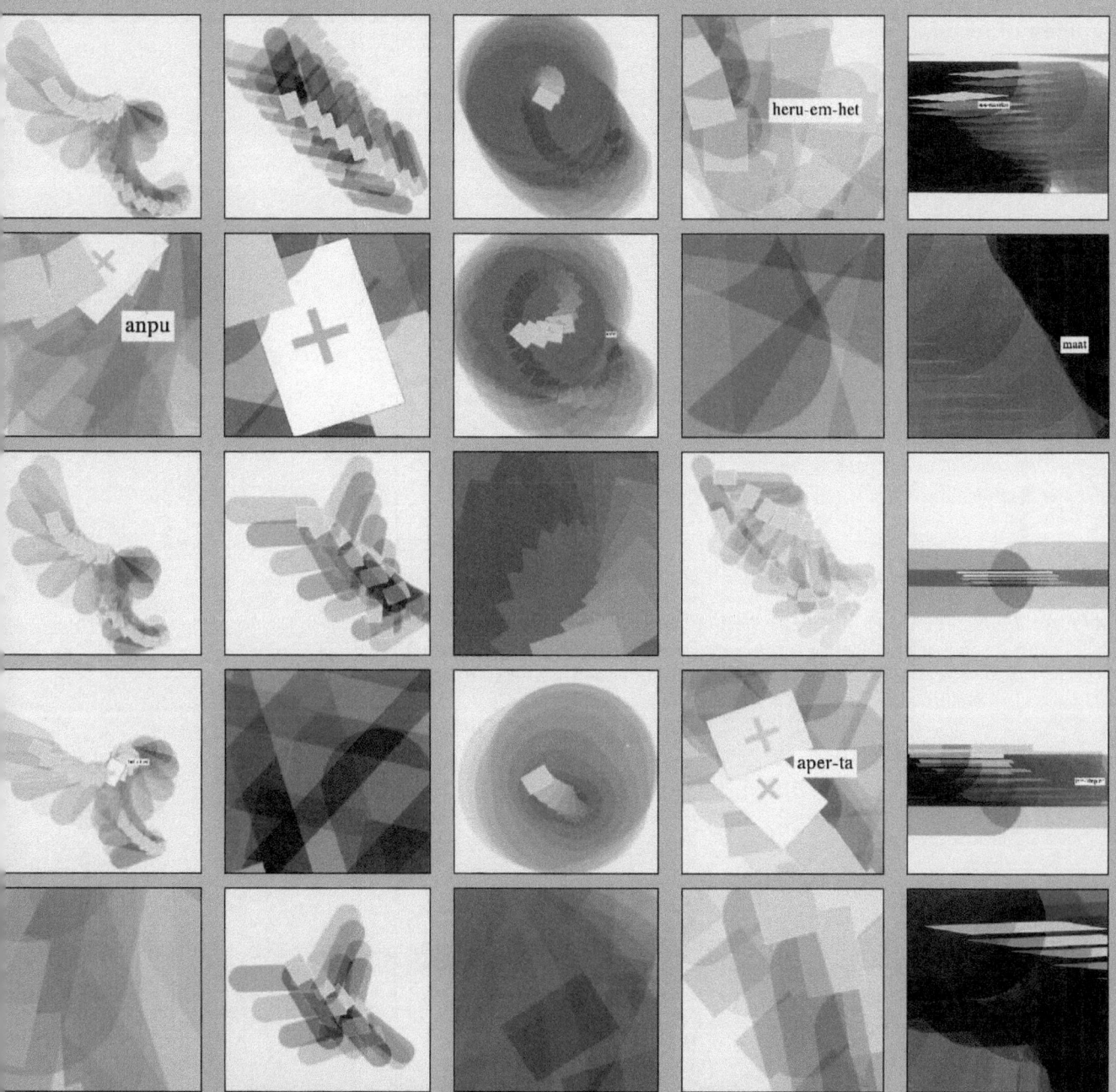

Wheels of fortune

As well as color and scaling changes the plotting positions of the movieclips have changed in variation 3a; these changes that been made in frame 2 are shown below. We now have a wheel of information.

```
with ( _root["unit" + i] ) {
    _y = Math.sin (i)* (50- Math.sqrt(i)*20)
    ➡ + Math.sin(i)+250;
    _x = Math.cos (i)*(50-Math.sqrt(i)*20) +
    ➡ Math.cos(i)+380;
    _rotation = i*60;
    _yscale = _xscale = 25+(i/4);
    inner.inner2.lineStyle(40,
    ➡ 0x6600FF*i/0.85, 30 );
    inner.inner2.moveTo(_parent._x,
    ➡_parent._y);
    inner.inner2.lineto(_parent._x-i,
    ➡_parent._y);
}
```

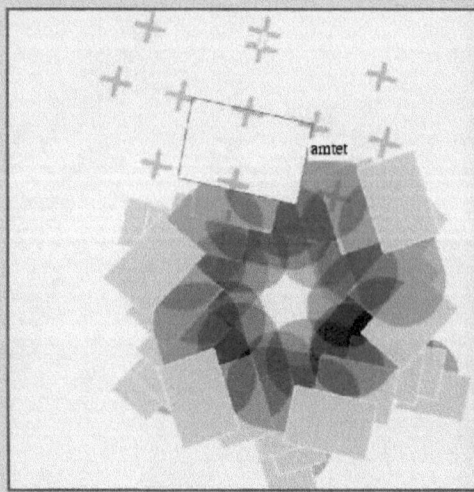

In 3b, the final configuration of the interface wheel is rendered static by removing any rotation on `inner` or `inner2`. Resembling a flower form, I thought it would be nice if the 'petals' fell off of the interface as they were clicked. This simultaneously lets us know what petal we've clicked on and aids the navigational sequence. I've done this by adding a few new lines to the `onRelease` event function in frame 1 and these are:

```
this.onEnterFrame = function () {
    if ( this._y < 600+random(20) ) {
        this._rotation-=10;
        this._y+=10;
    }
}
```

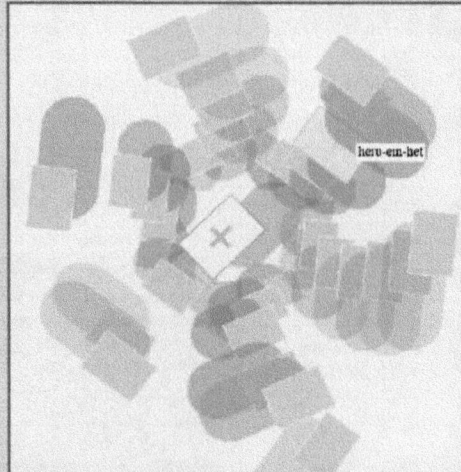

Variation 3c uses the same theme. Often, because of the animation, items become hidden behind other items in the interface. This type of interface would perhaps only be of use if there was a sequential hierarchy in which the information was to be read, such as pages in a book for example.

In the real world

Finally, I've given an example of this interface opening some Flash artwork I've produced. The work deals with ideas regarding structure and particle. As I've said before the line between interface and art in these files is often fine and I like it this way. Indeed the Flash files here have all been made from code based on these interface experiments. The `index.swf` loads up the interface, `rota_face_03a.swf` into `_level9` of the player. Clicking on a movieclip button then loads a specific SWF into `_level2` of the player – this means that the interface always appears above the content.

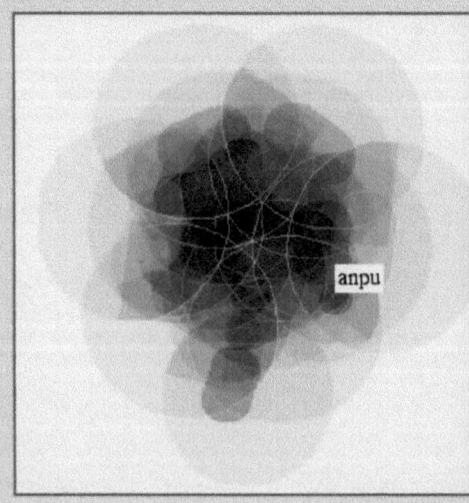

het-a-khet

Onwards

These interface experiments were produced during [some] days of rain in summer 2002, I think each could [benefit from] some extra development, however they serve their [purpose] as starting prototypes for something more. In a world [of] structured grid interfaces with rows and columns of buttons, though it would be fun and interesting to look at alternative formations for presenting links.

Perhaps the next move would be to develop a way of navigating through different levels in each of these interfaces using a graphical representation of the drill down method. Smaller modules of grouped buttons could be used in a recursive fashion. So, perhaps when you click on one button a new atoll of buttons would appear, each atoll representing successive layers or levels of information. Another obvious path to move down would be to link in an external data source, so the patterns of buttons would build up according to dynamic external data. Still further what about an interface that evolves aesthetically as it is being used? Better still, an interface whereby online users get to configure the interface themselves and leave a new formation of buttons for the next user who comes to the site.

Using the new MX way of adding events to movieclips in the timeline has allowed us to write organized and centralized code. The drawing API has given us the opportunity to make shapes on the screen as the Flash player runs eliminating the need for a library full of movieclips. A new set of objects such as the `textfield` object make tasks in Flash 5 that were pretty impossible very easy to accomplish in MX. The ability to import external media means we only have to wait for what we want to see or hear and not preload entire contents of Flash sites. More to the point, amends to sites can be carried out without even touching an FLA if we are only changing some JPGs for example. Because of these advances, and also because of enhancements to MX's internal compiling methods, file sizes for both FLAs and SWFs are considerably smaller than before. Indeed working on these files has afforded me the luxury of returning to floppy disks for backups!

From an artist-coder point of view, Flash is the most interesting tool on the planet, and this multi-dimensional design/development application just got a lot better with MX. With a lot of art made with computers, people quite often get obsessed with the idea that the technology is the message. As a creative tool, and by looking at some of the great work people are making with Flash, it seems so obvious that it's the personal showing through again and again to reveal truly great individual work. Not the case that it's the program that's talking. Flash MX has so many new elements to explore that by the time I will be just getting to grips with it, the new version of Flash will be out!

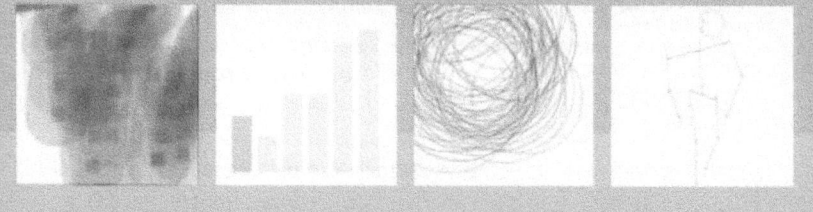

reacting to sound
ty lettau

The sight of sound

The first time that I really became interested in sound was during a trip to an antique store. While perusing the aisles, I noticed a small box. I was drawn to it because of the small graphic on the side. I picked it up and opened it. In the box was a roll of paper. Still curious, I began to unroll it and what I saw changed the way I think about things. I saw a pattern of holes cut into the paper. It was sort of like Braille, only much more complex, and clearly more linear. It was just a pattern of holes in paper, and I was amazed. I was amazed because the object was a reel for a player piano, and what I was looking at was a representation of a song. These holes were sound. I was actually looking at sound. I had seen wave patterns of sound before, but this was different. I think what made this interesting was that when I first saw it I had no idea what it was.

So began the journey into sound.

It also just so happens that a great friend of mine, Craig Kroeger (www.miniml.com) creates audio under the name Kemlus. I use his audio for almost everything I do. This project uses 6 of Craig's tracks. So thank you to Craig for allowing the use of those.

Anyway, what we are going to do here is to create several "engines" that generate patterns based on sound. The piano reel was actually a pattern that created sound. We are going to reverse this and use sound to create patterns and interactive toys.

FlashAmp

You may choose to skip this step as it requires you to download a piece of software. If you do not wish to purchase it, skip ahead to the next section.

For this all to work, we need a way to take our audio and translate it into numerical values which will represent the data in the audio. I use FlashAmp which can be downloaded at www.marmalademedia.com.au/flashamp/download.htm. It costs $30.00, but in my opinion it is well worth it. You can download a demo version, but it will only let you record a small portion of audio which isn't enough to use. If you want to get into this, the $30.00 is a small price for what it can do for you. If you don't think that it is something you will use often, I suggest skipping this step and simply using my prerecorded files. You can do this entire chapter with the files provided, but if you want to customize it for your own use or if

you want to use this idea on a project, you will need to buy FlashAmp.

There are other utilities to use. If you are using another utility to record data, this process will be slightly different and you will need to figure it out on your own. I am not familiar with all of the software for doing this, but most software comes with documentation. If you can find a free application that does this, or if you already have one, it should tell you how to use it.

Source audio files (01.aiff, 02.aiff, 03.aiff, 04.aiff, 05.aiff, 06.aiff)...

To start, we will need several sound files (here we use six). I typically use AIFF format audio and compress in Flash, but we can use anything. We *will* need an AIFF format for FlashAmp data recording later, so it's easier to start with AIFF files; I've named mine "01.aiff" – "06.aiff". If you wish to try your own audio, find six audio files and name them the same way.

Being that these audio files are very large, I have only included one of the AIFF files and one of the FLA files for the audio. To do this first step in full, you will need to find or create five more audio files.

Open FlashAmp and follow the steps using the settings below

Select an Audio File: "01.aiff"
Amplitude List: Yes (Checkmark)
Cue Point Name List: No (X)
Frames Per Second: "15"
Value Scale: "100"
Smoothing: Yes (Checkmark)
Save FlashAmp File: Name it "01.as"

Other settings will produce other results. For example, setting the FPS to 90 will give a smoother data scale with much more data, but it will choke Flash. Feel free to experiment with the values, but for now, keep them as shown above.

Data files (01.as, 02.as, 03.as, 04.as, 05.as, 06.as)...

FlashAmp will write a text file. If we open it, we see this:

```
amplitude = (100,86,63,58,55,53,49,49,48,
.......49,32,0) &ampDone=1
```

We now have a list of values, separated by commas (convenient, seeing as this is how arrays are structured in Flash) that range from 0 to 100. These numbers represent the volume of the audio from start to finish.

We need to make a few changes to the text file in order to use this file how we want to. First, change the variable name from "amplitude" to "amp". We do this so that later in Flash it will be easier to refer to. Next, add the code to make it into an array. We write "new Array" in front of the parentheses to declare that what follows is an array. Lastly, we remove ampDone=1.

```
amp = new Array
(100,86,63,58,55,53,49,49,48,.......49,32,0)
```

Save the file. Now we have a usable array that Flash can understand. Remember in FlashAmp when it asked for the filename to save as? We added the suffix .AS to it. This stands for ActionScript and will signal Flash (along with the method we use to bring the data in) that this is to be read into the ActionScript of the movie.

Repeat this process for all six audio clips, so we end with 6 text files named 01.as – 06.as.

Flash audio files(01.fla, 02.fla, 03.fla, 04.fla, 05.fla, 06.fla)...

We have our sound file, and from it we have recorded our data file. So now we need to get into Flash. Open Flash and make a new file. It doesn't matter what size the stage is. The only thing that matters about the movie is the Frames Per Second. Set it to 15 because that is what FPS our data file was recorded at. Save the file as "01.fla".

If at any time, we load in any movie with a FPS lower than 15, everything will slow. To remedy this, we just need to be sure that all files with a frame rate are set to 15.

Now we need to import the "01.aiff" file. From the library, bring up the audio info and apply the following settings:

Compression: MP3
Bit Rate: 16 kbps
Quality: Best

Again, this is what I use. Try different settings to see what they do.

Next, we need to create two layers in this movie. Call one 'Audio' and the other 'Actions'. In frame 1 on the Audio layer, add the sound. Set the sound properties in Flash as follows:

Sync: Stream
Loop: 0 times

Now, extend the frames in this layer out by adding blank frames until you see the end of the sound. A streaming sound will only play while there are frames there for it to play on. In order to stream the sound, we need to extend the frames. If we don't, the sound will stop. Basically, streaming sound means that Flash isn't downloading all of the sound before it plays. It starts playing and downloads as it goes. This makes the download quicker (a huge benefit) but this is not the reason we use this method. Flash handles streaming sound by playing through frames. Imagine that the frames and the sound extend in the same way so that if the playhead is on the 140th frame, the sound is also at the 140th "frame". The exact reason that we are using streaming sound and frame passage will become clear a little later, so for now, let's just move on.

Go back to frame 1 and select the Actions layer. On frame 1, add this code:

```
#include("04.as")
```

We don't need any other code here anyway, but for further reference, do not ever put another action on a frame with an #include command. It needs to be alone.

This code is the other part of Flash understanding that the data file is actually ActionScript. The #include command tells Flash that the text it is importing is valid ActionScript. If there is a problem in the code syntax of the 01.as file, the Flash file will reflect the error. If we encounter a problem later on, it is best to first check the data file. It can be easy to make syntactical errors in it. It is also important to note that the #include command operates on export, not in real time. As long as the data file is there for Flash to call to it doesn't need to be there anymore. For example, if you upload to a web server, you do not need to upload the 01.as file, as it is already a part of the Flash file.

We can now export the movie by pressing Command/Control and Return. Since we named it 01.fla, our exported file will be 01.swf.

Now repeat this process to create six individual FLA files and export them all to individual SWF files. Be sure that you replace the audio clip being imported *and* the #include command.

Main files...

Everything that we have created thus far will become our audio library. No matter which file we are working on, we will draw from this library of six audio tracks. Note that if you are creating your own audio, you should now have 24 files (six AIFF files, six AS files, six SWF files and six FLA files). Also note that I only have 14 (one AIFF file, six AS files, six SWF files and one FLA file) because the FLA and the AIFF files get big and there isn't room for them all.

In this chapter, we are going to be creating 3 different experiments in sound. They will be named by letter (A,B,C). So let's get started on A.

We are starting off with different sound files in each project. The defaults are:

A = 04.swf
B = 03.swf
C = Random (and an interface to select tracks)

Project A (The Basic Engine)...

Now that we have the entire framework in place, we can finally create our main Flash movie. Make a new file and save it as A_01.fla.

FPS: "15"
Size: "400 x 400"

Create two layers and call them 'Objects' and 'Actions'. We will be writing *all* of the code for this movie on the Actions layer in frame 1 unless otherwise noted. To save time, if we are writing code and we haven't specified an alternate location for it, then we are writing it here. Let's start with some parameters:

```
_quality="low";
fscommand(allowscale="false");
loadMovieNum("audio/04.swf",10);
stop();
```

Most of this is quite self-explanatory. _quality="low" simply sets the movie quality to non-anti-aliased. fscom-

mand(allowscale="false") makes the movie unscalable. The next line is what we have been doing all of the othe steps for. loadMovieNum("audio/04.swf",10) brings the audio.swf file into the main movie. Notice we are loading it on level 10.

We need to take a moment to understand the hierarchy at work here. The key to this whole process is the array called amp which houses all of our volume data. This array (called 'amp') exists in the data file called 04.as. Since we used #include to add the data file when we exported 04.swf the amp array is now in the 04.swf file. Finally, since we just loaded in 04.swf into the main movie on level 10, our amp array is now on level 10 in relation to the main movie. So we want to call to this array to retrieve or use the values in it, we will say _level10.amp[?].

Finally, we end the frame passage of the main timeline by saying stop(). We do this for performance reasons. It takes Flash more energy to chug through frames than it does to run code, so all of our motion will occur with loops and clipEvents.

Now we need to add a fair amount of code to what we just wrote.

```
_quality="low";
fscommand(allowscale="false");
loadMovieNum("audio/04.swf",10);
stop();

this.onEnterFrame=function() {
    if (C<_level10.amp.length) {
        C++;
    } else {
        C=0;
    }
};
```

The first part of this code is to declare a loop function this.onEnterFrame=function() is actually a lot simpler than it looks. this simply declares that the target is the _root level. So anything that happens in this loop will be relative to the _root level. onEnterFrame is just like the Flash 5 syntax of MC clipEvents. The only difference that now Flash MX can remotely target a clipEvent without the code actually being on the objects. Lastly, we need to declare a blank function() to hold all of the code that we want to happen.

emember that although everything in this movie is ...opped, the `04.swf` on level 10 is actually cycling real ...ames.

...e also need to understand frame passage. The first set of ...ode included a `stop()` to pause the `_root` timeline's ...layhead. But `onEnterFrame` doesn't mean literally that it ...eeds to pass frames, it just means that 15 times per second ...because our movie is at 15 FPS), this code is going to ...xecute.

...o, every time the movie cycles through a frame (specifical-..., on the entrance of that frame), the `_root` timeline will ...nlist a function and run all of the code inside of it.

...ow, let's look at the next part; the `if` statement simply ...ives us a conditional situation. When something is true, do ...art A; otherwise, do part B. All we need now is to ...etermine what that something is. We need to create a ...ounter which will cycle through the entire amp array. This ...ounter will eventually be used to extract the corresponding ...alue from the amp array. Think of it like this: every frame ...hat passes is a frame that the `04.swf` file has passed ...hrough. So we need a way to keep a counter in the main ...ovie that will coincide with the frame of audio that ...4.swf is on. If we look at the `if` statement, we see that ...ur condition set so that if some value named `C` is less than ...he length of the "amp" array, then the code runs. `C` will be ...ur counter variable. If we look to where it says C++, we see ...here `C` counts. C++ means that each frame, `C` will increase ...y one (this is called "incremental"). So each "frame", `C` is a ...alue one higher than it was the last frame. Also, as `C` ...ounts, `04.swf` on level 10 also plays real frames. So on the ...20th frame cycle of the main movie, level 10 is at real ...ame 220 and `C` equals 220.

...ur movie will do this until the number that `C` represents is ...reater than the amount of values in the amp array (repre-...ented by the property `.length`). `_level10.amp.length` ...neans that we look to level 10, find amp and see how long ... is. When `C` is greater than this, we do something else.

...ince amp is an array, the length is the amount of ...alues in it, not the amount of characters. If we ...rite `varMyName="SoundOfDesign"` and then find ...arMyName.length, we will get a result of 13 because it ...ounts characters if the target is a variable.

The something else that we need to do is to reset `C` to 0. When the `C` value is greater than the length of the amp array, we also know that `audio.swf` on level 10 will be out of frames. When streaming audio runs out of frames, it restarts. When the audio restarts, we need `C` to restart, thereby also restarting where we call into the amp array to the beginning.

OK, we have the overall code structure in place, but there are a few more steps to go. Before we write any more code, we will need to make an object that we can later set to *react* to the audio. But even before we do this, let's discuss how this is all happening. We are going to make a movie clip in a moment. We are then going to control the properties (such as `_x`, `_y`, etc.) of this MC. To control these properties, we aren't actually using the audio stream, but rather the data in the "amp" array. The "amp" array, and the values in it, are directly related to the volume of the audio on any given part of the audio stream. So we can make the movie clip look as though the audio is affecting it, when it is actually the array values that are affecting it.

Let's make a 4x4 square of any color. Do not put a stroke on it. Make it into a movie clip by pressing F8. Name it 'MC_Clip'. Next, select the movie clip and give it an instance name of 'Clip'. Place the clip on the stage using the info palette. Set it to $X = 0$, $Y = 0$. Before we move on, let's also set the MC's `_alpha` to 25%. This will help later. Now we have an object that is ready to be given instructions.

Add the following line to the code we have written already:

```
_quality="low";
   fscommand(allowscale="false");
   loadMovieNum("audio/04.swf",10);
   stop();

this.onEnterFrame=function() {
   if (C<_level10.amp.length) {
      C++;
      Clip._y=_level10.amp[_level10.
➥_currentframe];
   } else {
      C=0;
   }
};
```

This will finally give us an object that reacts. It is very simple at this point. All it does is move up and down based on the data, though it appears as though the volume is actually moving it. Also note that we aren't even using the C counter yet. We need that framework in place, but the _y position is controlled by another value. Notice that we are setting the _y to look at level 10, find "amp" and extract a value. The value is not C (as we might expect), but rather, _currentframe. The reason we do this is to ensure that we are calling to the *exact* part of the array that the audio is on. The frame that audio.swf on level 10 is on represents the exact part of the audio that is playing. So, if we use that to get the array value, we ensure that the array value is the right one. If we use C and the audio lags a bit or some other discrepancy occurs, the two will not be in sync. Also note that to call into an array, we use square brackets. Whatever is inside these brackets is the part of the array that is drawn out. So if level 10 is on the 160th frame, then the 159th value in the array is being drawn. Arrays operate on zero scale. This means that the 1st member of the array is actually the 0th member. So calling to the 160th wil actually bring up the 159th.

After writing this, save and export. (The file should be very much like A_01.fla)

Again, again!

Now that we have the basic movement in place, we can go in many different directions. In order for this to serve our purposes, we need to spruce it up a bit more. To do this, we have options. The best course of action at this point (read: what will give up the best potential for experimentation later) is to create a small replication engine so that we can affect more than just one MC. Let's add two new lines of code, and let's also change the last one we added.

```
_quality="low";
fscommand(allowscale="false");
loadMovieNum("audio/04.swf",10);
stop();

this.onEnterFrame=function() {
    if (C<_level10.amp.length) {
        C++;
        // Replicate
        Clip.duplicateMovieClip("Clip"+C,C);
        _root["Clip"+C]._x=C;
        _root["Clip"+C]._y=_level10.amp[_level10._currentframe];
    } else {
        C=0;
    }
};
```

Again, we have added code which *looks* more confusing than it *is*. The first new line simply tells "Clip" to duplicate. Notice we are finally using C. We need to use C for two reasons. The first involves the first part of the parentheses. We say Clip.duplicateMovieClip() to duplicate the movie clip. This gives us a new movie clip every time we run this line. But we need to consider the parameters of the new duplicate. Inside the parentheses exist to parameters which can be expressed as (what we want to name the new clip, what depth the new clip goes onto). If we want to duplicate a movie clip, we can't name the duplicate the xact same thing as the original. So we need to change its name. If we only wanted one uplicate, we could just call it 'Clip2'. But, we want to continually make duplicates. This is hy we created C. As C counts, duplicates are being made. Notice in the first part of the arentheses it says "Clip"+C. This means that we are using the string "Clip" as a literal erm. But we are also adding (the + means append whatever is next to the end of the string Clip") the C value. So the first duplicated movie clip is called 'Clip1' and the second is alled 'Clip2' and so on. This serves the need for unique naming. Next we need to determine he new duplicate's depth. Depth is like a level of the movie but is within the main movie. o far, we have the main movie on level 0 and the audio.swf file on level 10. When we uplicate a movie clip, it creates layers of depth in level 0. To duplicate a movie clip, we *must* ut it on a new level, and we *must not* use a level already taken. If we do, we will overwrite rhat was there. Also, if we duplicate 100 movie clips, the 80th is on depth 80, but is still elow level 10 because depth is all within level 0. As for depth and levels, the higher the umber the more in front it is. So by using C as the depth we get a unique depth every frame ust as we got a unique name.

ow what we have is objects being replicated constantly, all ready to react to the audio. We an do this one of two ways. We can set the movie based on the audio just when it loads, or e can set it to always follow the audio data. Before, when we just had one clip, it was always ooking to the data and updating. This time we are going to set each clip just when it loads.

o call to the clips as they are made, and to call to them only once, we again use C. We say root["Clip"+C]._x to call to the duplicate that was just made. If we think about how C ehaves; that is that it counts up, but on any given frame is the same value for the entirety f that one frame, we can more easily understand this. We just used C to name the dupli- ate. On the 40th frame, C is 40 so the duplicate is named 'Clip40' and is on a depth of 40. Vhen the movie gets done doing this, the movie has other code to run before it recycles nd changes C to the next increment. So when the movie hits _root["Clip"+C]._x, C is till 40. So this line of code really just reads _root.Clip40._x. This means for that frame lip40 is being affected, just once. Then the next frame, C will have counted to 41 and there- ore Clip40 is no longer the same as _root["Clip"+C] because that now means Clip41. This s just a way to apply and run this code on each clip as it loads and then leave it alone.

Ve target our clip with _root["Clip"+C]._x and we set it to C. Since C is counting, each ime a clip is made, it will be one pixel farther to the right than the one before it. So now ve have what appears to be movie clips replicating across the screen.

Ve edit the _y property to target the same as the _x code did, and we leave the value the ame and we are left with... _root["Clip"+C]._y=level10.amp[_level10._current- rame];

ave a new version as 'A_02.fla' and export, (or look at our file A_02.fla). We now see a ot more happening. We are now basically tracking the audio and creating a map of it.

Between the lines

At this point, we are starting to see something that has potential. For the next iteration, we will try to utilize some of the new features of Flash to add to our project. First, let's try a simple Line Method.

```
_quality="low";
fscommand(allowscale="false");
loadMovieNum("audio/04.swf",10);
stop();

this.onEnterFrame=function() {
    if (C<_level10.amp.length) {
        C++;
        // Replicate
        Clip.duplicateMovieClip("Clip"+C,C);
        _root["Clip"+C]._x=C;
        _root["Clip"+C]._y=_level10.amp[_level10._currentframe];
        // Draw Lines
        this.createEmptyMovieClip("Draw", C+100000);
        Draw.lineStyle(.25, 0xFF3399, 25);
        Draw.moveTo(_root["Clip"+C]._x, _root["Clip"+C]._y);
        Draw.lineTo(_root["Clip"+(C-1)]._x, _root["Clip"+(C-1)]._y);
    } else {
        C=0;
    }
};
```

Yet again, we have added code that isn't very complicated once we understand how it works. The Draw features are new to Flash MX. Thus, they require a bit more imagination than what we were used to in Flash 5. The main reason why this is different is because Flash is actually *creating* a shape on the fly.

First, we need to create a movie clip for this shape to be stored. We could just make a MC by hand, but for this purpose, creating one through code works well. We create a MC by writing `this.createEmptyMovieClip("Draw", C+100000)`. This works very much like how we duplicated an MC earlier. We choose a name and a depth, and that's it. Notice that we add 100000 to the depth. We do this because if we use C, we will overwrite the Clip movie clips. Adding 100000 insures that the line being drawn is well out of the range of possible Clip movie clip depths. Next, we need to supply information for Flash to use as the line style. `Draw.lineStyle(.25, 0xFF3399, 25)` declares that we are talking about the movie clip Draw and any parameters within the parentheses will apply to that movie clip. We have three parameters to fill in. They are stroke, color, and alpha. The next two lines control the positioning of the line to be drawn. These are little more than a start point and an end point and then Flash connects the dots. `Draw.moveTo(_root["Clip"+C]._x, _root["Clip"+C]._y)` declares the current Clip movie clip as the start point. There are two values because we need to declare both the _x and the _y. `Draw.lineTo(_root["Clip"+(C-1)]._x, _root["Clip"+(C-1)]._y)` is what actually makes the line and connects the dots.

Each time this code cycles, it enters the Draw movie clip and adds the next line segment. Save a new version as 'A_03.fla' and export. (or see our version of the file `A_03.fla`). We see this:

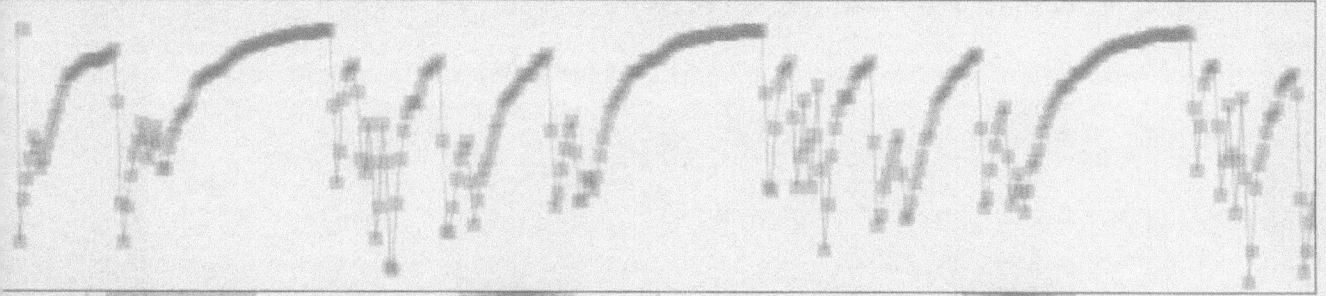

We can also set the alpha of the Clip movie clips to 0% which will leave only the lines of the Draw movie clip visible, like this:

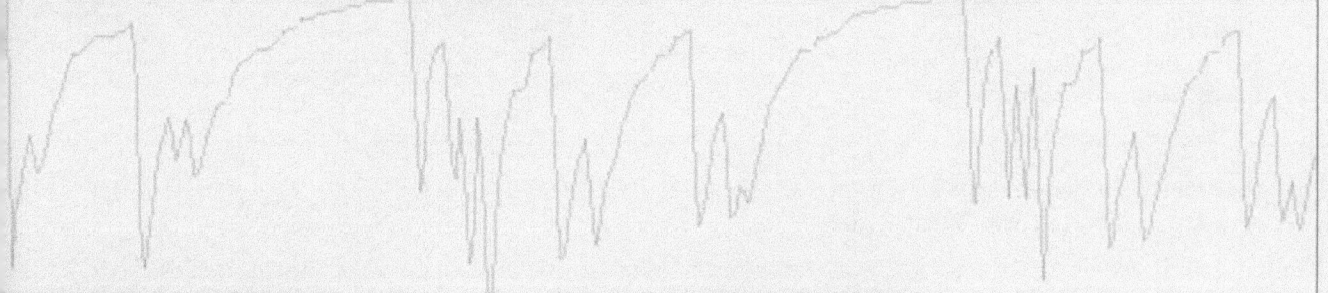

We can also start to randomize a bit so that the placement is determined by the audio, but it isn't as precise:

```
_quality="low";
fscommand(allowscale="false");
loadMovieNum("audio/04.swf",10);
stop();

this.onEnterFrame=function() {
    if (C<_level10.amp.length) {
        C++;
        // Replicate
        Clip.duplicateMovieClip("Clip"+C,C);
        _root["Clip"+C]._x=C+(Math.random(20)-10);
        _root["Clip"+C]._y=_level10.amp[_level10._currentframe]+(Math.random(20)-10);
        // Draw Lines
        this.createEmptyMovieClip("Draw", C+100000);
        Draw.lineStyle(.25, 0xFF3399, 25);
        Draw.moveTo(_root["Clip"+C]._x, _root["Clip"+C]._y);
        Draw.lineTo(_root["Clip"+(C-1)]._x, _root["Clip"+(C-1)]._y);
    } else {
        C=0;
    }
};
```

All we have to do is to declare a range for the random to choose from. The value returned will be between 0 and 19 (Math.random() is a zero based scale also) and then we minus 10. This gives us equal probability that the number will be positive versus negative. Adding this random range to the placement on both axes gives us a bit more of a chaotic map.

Next, a simple change in the stroke weight and alpha yields a different result.

```
_quality="low";
fscommand(allowscale="false");
loadMovieNum("audio/04.swf",10);
stop();

this.onEnterFrame=function() {
    if (C<_level10.amp.length) {
        C++;
        // Replicate
        Clip.duplicateMovieClip("Clip"+C,C);
        _root["Clip"+C]._x=C+(Math.random(20)-10);
        _root["Clip"+C]._y=_level10.amp[_level10._currentframe]
                                            +(Math.random(20)-10);
        // Draw Lines
        this.createEmptyMovieClip("Draw", C+100000);
        Draw.lineStyle(20, 0xFF3399, 10);
        Draw.moveTo(_root["Clip"+C]._x, _root["Clip"+C]._y);
        Draw.lineTo(_root["Clip"+(C-1)]._x, _root["Clip"+(C-1)]._y);
    } else {
        C=0;
    }
};
```

Feel free to experiment doing different things.

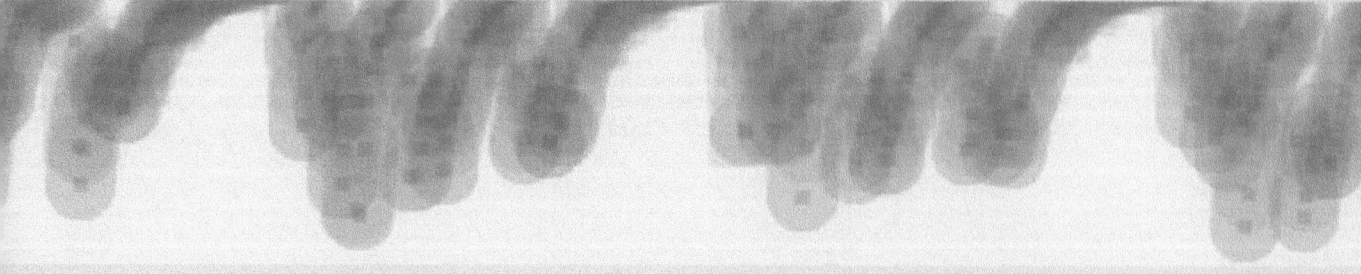

The equalizer

Before we move on to a completely different project, let's use this engine to build a quick equalizer. It isn't a true equalizer in that it is only using volume as its guide, but it is better than the arbitrarily tweened animations that we see often enough. Let's start by changing our code a bit.

```
_quality = "low";
fscommand(allowscale="false");
loadMovieNum("audio/02.swf", 10);
stop();
//
this.onEnterFrame = function() {
    if (C<6) {
        C++;
        // Replicate
        Clip.duplicateMovieClip("Clip"+C,C);
        Clip1._alpha = 25;
        _root["Clip"+C]._x=(C*5)+186;
        _root["Clip"+C]._y=200;
    } else {
        C = 0;
    };
};
```

We are loading in a new audio clip. Then we adjust the counter to only loop through six values instead of hundreds (stated before as the length of the array). Since we are now making only six duplicates, we reset C every 6th pass, thus the entire engine is very compact because of the x value. `_root["Clip"+C]._x=(C*5)+186` uses the C value times 5 (our clip is 4 pixels wide, so C x 5 moves each subsequent duplicate over one pixel past the last one). Then we add 186 to keep it all centered. We do this because our equalizer is 28 pixels wide and our movie is 400 pixels wide, so the center is 200. If we halve the equalizer, we get 14. 200 − 14 = 186. Last, we set the y axis to 200.

`Clip1._alpha = 25` just keeps the first clip in the line at 25% alpha. Now is a good time to change the physical alpha of Clip to 10% so that the other five will be lighter. We do this because the first one is reacting real-time and the other five are subsequently behind. This way, it is more obvious what the "master" level bar is.

Now all we do is write a few lines on the "Clip" MC:

```
onClipEvent (load) {
        C = _root.C;
}
onClipEvent (enterFrame) {
        _yscale = _level10.amp[_level10._currentframe-C]*10;
}
```

All the load `ClipEvent` does is to localize the C value to the MC. As C changes on the root, we want each duplicate to know what C was when it was "born". Then we set the `_yscale` property to the audio level times 10. As we target the frame to pull from the "amp" array, we minus C, because each duplicate understands its own C as something different from the others. C acts as an identifier for each MC. So by subtracting C, we ensure that each movie clip is getting a different value from the array. For example, the 5th duplicate is actually getting a value 5 less than what the amp array is actually on. If the `_currentframe` of `_level10` is 230, then the 5th duplicate is actually pulling the 225th value because it has subtracted its own C (5).

Lastly, we need to double-click into "Clip" and set the center point to Y = -4. This way, as we adjust the `_yscale`, the center point is on the bottom and will therefore scale upward. Finally, place Clip somewhere off the stage. It doesn't matter where, just anywhere outside the boundary of the stage. We can also write `_visible = 0` which is 'cleaner' but i'ts also more code. It's up to you. There are so many different ways to do the same thing in Flash, it's really just a matter of preference. I try to write code so that I need the fewest lines possible, but you may wish to do things differently. Again, try experimenting and moving things round to see what they do.

Save a new version as 'A_04.fla' and export. (or refer to the file A_04.fla).

Before we move on, let's try one more thing. Make a square 8 x 8 pixels in size. Make it a button and name it 'NavButton'. On this button, add the ActionScript:

```
on (release) {
    loadMovieNum("audio/0"+MyNumber+".swf", 10);
}
```

Now, select the button and make it into a movie clip. Nam it 'NavMC'. Select the movie clip and give it an instanc name of 'Nav'. Then, on the root create an Actions laye and add this:

```
_quality = "low";
fscommand(allowscale="false");
loadMovieNum("audio/02.swf", 10);
this.onLoad = function() {
    for (N=1; N<7; N++) {
        // Replicate
        Nav.duplicateMovieClip("Nav"+N, N+100)
        _root["Nav"+N]._x = (N*11)+156;
        _root["Nav"+N].MyNumber = N;
    }
};
stop();
//
this.onEnterFrame = function() {
    if (C<6) {
        C++;
        // Replicate
        Clip.duplicateMovieClip("Clip"+C,C);
        Clip1._alpha = 25;
        _root["Clip"+C]._x=(C*5)+186;
        _root["Clip"+C]._y=200;
    } else {
        C = 0;
    };
};
```

Now the MC we just made will duplicate across th screen to form six buttons. The key here `_root["Nav"+N].MyNumber = N`. This tells each duplicat as it is created, what number it is. Remember on the butto when we wrote `loadMovieNum("audio/0"+MyNumber+".swf"` 10)? This makes each button load a different audio cl because each button's host movie clip knows itself to be different number than the rest.

Save a new version as 'A_05.fla' and export. (or refer to th file A_05.fla). All this did was give us a more versati equalizer because we can now test different audio clips o the fly.

  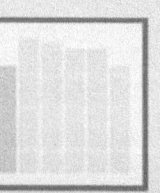   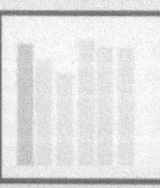 

Project B (The enhanced Engine)

For the next project, we are going to take a look into the intro toy that I built for www.cymbalbranding.com. It utilizes audio reactivity in a bit more of a unique and interactive way. What is interesting about this is that it reacts to *both* the audio *and* to the user.

This project will go in a different direction from that which Project A did, but we will be using a lot of the same setup and a lot of the same code as Project A. If anything that follows is confusing, refer back to Project A.

To get set up, keep the same stage settings as Project A, Save a new file called 'B_01.fla'. Create another instance of the movie clip Clip. Now we should have two movie clips on the stage, both instances of Clip. Rename one of them 'Origin' and the other 'Drag'. Place Drag at x=200, y=100 and place Origin at x=300 and y=200.

Then, in the Actions layer, change the script to read as so.

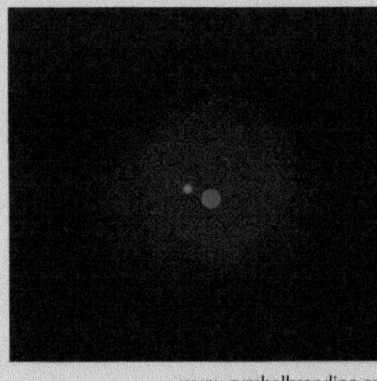

www.cymbalbranding.com

```
_quality = "low";
fscommand(allowscale="false");
loadMovieNum("audio/03.swf", 10);
stop();

this.onEnterFrame = function() {
    // Dragger
    if (MD) {
        _root.Drag._x = _root._xmouse;
    }
    // Elastic Engine
    TXn = (TXn*.95)+(_root.Drag._x-_root.Origin._x)*.025;
    _root.Origin._x += TXn;
    _root.Origin._y = _root.Drag._y + (_level10.amp[_level10._currentframe]*2)+TXn;
    // Draw Lines
    this.createEmptyMovieClip("Draw", C+100000);
    Draw.lineStyle(.25, 0xFF3399, 25);
    Draw.moveTo(_root.Origin._x, _root.Origin._y);
    Draw.lineTo(_root.Drag._x, _root.Drag._y);
};
this.onMouseDown = function() {
    MD = 1;
};
this.onMouseUp = function() {
    MD = 0;
};
```

This is what all of the setup code looks like for Project B. If we look this over a bit, we will see some new things that we haven't talked about yet. We will also see some familiar code, so let's look more closely at this.

The first thing that is different is that we are loading in a different audio clip. We can change this to any value from 01 to 06 to try our different audio clips.

The next thing that is different is that we have completely removed the C counter variable from Project A. This project will be using just one instance of Clip so we do not need any duplication (yet).

If we look down to the end of the code, we will see the addition of two new event functions. We are setting a variable called MD based on the behavior of the mouse. When the left mouse button is down, MD = 1, when it's up, MD = 0. Basically, this gives us a conditional situation that will allow us to tell if the mouse is pressed or not by looking to MD. Now if we look to the top again (under the comment //Dragger), we see how and why we use this. The line _root.Drag._x = _root._xmouse is triggered when MD is true. Any value (including 1) will read as true, so when the mouse is down, MD = 1 and therefore, _root.Drag._x = _root._xmouse. So, when the mouse is pressed, the movie clip Drag will follow the mouse on the x axis.

Now that we have this dragging mechanism in place, we need to use it to affect something else. The next part of the code does just that (under the comment //Elastic Engine). For this, we are going to make Origin follow Drag by controlling the y axis with the audio and the x axis with this code.

Let's look into the x axis first. We see two lines that control the x axis. We have a variable and a property being set. TXn = (TXn*.95)+(_root.Drag._x-_root.Origin._x)*.025 is probably the most complex single line of code in here. This is what gives us the calculation for the elastic motion.

We could also write TXn=(TXn*F)+(_root.Drag._x-_root.Origin._x)*V. This might help keep track of what the decimal values do. Think of F as *friction*, or how long the MC will take to come to rest after it is agitated. Think of V as *velocity*, or how fast the MC moves. Then we would need to declare F = .95 and D = .025 in the code. The closer to 1 each value gets, the faster (in the case of V) and the longer (in the case of F) it will be. It takes more lines of code this way, but it might be easier to track. Also, try playing with these values. There's nothing like experimentation to aid learning!

Is easier to understand this if we break it into manageable parts. _root.Drag._x-_root.Origin._x is merely the distance between the two movie clips. This distance can be positive or negative, but at this point, that is what we need. "Origin" is at 20 and "Drag" is at 100, then we are left with this simplified equation:

TXn = (TXn*.95)+(100-20)*.025 or TXn = (TXn*.95)+(80)*.025

Flash uses the same rules that govern any math equation; calculations in parentheses come first. Now let's look at the TXn*.95 part. This is really just a way to shave a bit off of the current value of TXn. Variables default to 0, so the first time we use it without setting it, TXn equals 0. So if TXn was 0, then 0 * .95 is 0. So now we have TXn = (0)+(80)*.025. The next calculation will be 80 * .025, resulting in 2. TXn = (0)+2 is what is left and we can see that TXn will equal 2. _root.Origin._x += TXn just adds TXn to the x location of Origin. So 2 will be added to Origin thereby making its new x location 22.

Now, to see the behavior in action, let's run it through again. Now TXn is 2, so 2 * .95 is 1.9, and the new locations are 22 and 100, so now we have TXn = (1.9)+(78)*.025. The next calculation will be 78 * .025, resulting in 1.95. TXn = (1.9)+1.95 is what is left and we can see that TXn will equal 3.85. Now Origin is at 25.85 and TXn is at 3.85

Let's run it through one more time. Now TXn is 3.85, so 3.85 * .95 is 3.65, and the new locations are 25.85 and 100, so now we have TXn = (3.85)+(74.15)*.025. The next calculation will be 74.15 x .025, resulting in about 1.85. TXn = (3.85)+ 1.85 is what is left and we can see that TXn will equal around 5.7.

After three iterations, we can start to see the behavior. The closer the two MCs get, the larger the distance that "Origin" will move each "frame". This is why, as they get farther away from one another, "Origin" goes less distance each "frame" and appears to slow down. They do this until the distance that they jump becomes opposite (like positive to negative), at which point, "Origin" starts to come back toward "Drag".

The next step is to set the y location. _root.Origin._y = _root.Drag._y+(_level10.amp[_level10._current-frame]*2)+TXn simply sets the y location of Origin to whatever y location Drag is at, then adds the level of the audio times two and then adds TXn. The addition of TXn is merely to add a bit of imperfection into the movement.

Finally, we apply the line drawing code the same as in Project A.

Save this and export (or refer to the file B_01.fla). We can see that we have two connected points and one reacts to the audio while the other can be dragged.

Circles in the sound

For the next addition, we are going to make another movie clip. This is going to be a rather complex clip, so let's do it one step at a time. Make a circle with no fill and a hairline stroke. Create a movie clip out of this and set the registration point to center, and name it 'Node3'. Now, select this clip. It does not need an instance name, so leave that blank. Make this movie clip into another and again set the registration point to center, and this time name it 'Node2'. Select this clip. It too, needs no instance name. Double-click into Node2 (which now has Node3 inside of it). Select Node3 and move it up 10 pixels. Click back out to the root level. Now select Node2 and make it into yet another movie clip. Set the registration point again to center and name this 'Node1'. Select it and give it an instance name of 'Node'. Now double-click into Node1. Duplicate the keyframe at frame 1 to frame 12. Select frame 1 and set it to a motion tween with a clockwise rotation of 1. The reason why we moved Node3 up 10 pixels inside of Node2 was so that when we tween Node2 inside of Node1 and install the rotation, it will wobble.

Now that our movie clip is ready, add a few lines (which will look familiar) to the code on the root in the layer "Actions".

```
_quality = "low";
fscommand(allowscale="false");
loadMovieNum("audio/03.swf", 10);
stop();

this.onEnterFrame = function() {
    // Replicate
    if (C<59) {
        _root.Node.duplicateMovieClip("Node"+C, C);
        C++;
    }
    // Dragger
    if (MD) {
        _root.Drag._x = _root._xmouse;
    }
    // Elastic Engine
    TXn = (TXn*.95)+(_root.Drag._x-_root.Origin._x)*.025;
    _root.Origin._x += TXn;
    _root.Origin._y = _root.Drag._y +
                     (_level10.amp[_level10._currentframe]*2)+TXn;
    // Draw Lines
    this.createEmptyMovieClip("Draw", C+100000);
    Draw.lineStyle(.25, 0xFF3399, 25);
    Draw.moveTo(_root.Origin._x, _root.Origin._y);
    Draw.lineTo(_root.Drag._x, _root.Drag._y);
};
this.onMouseDown = function() {
    MD = 1;
};
this.onMouseUp = function() {
    MD = 0;
};
```

We should remember this from before. If not, look back to Project A. The only difference is that we aren't resetting C, so this loop happens only once.

Lastly, to make this iteration complete, we need to apply a few actions to the "Node" MC.

```
onClipEvent (load) {
    _x = _root.Origin._x;
    _y = _root.Origin._y;
}

onClipEvent (enterFrame) {
    _x -= (_x-_root.Origin._x)/(random(20)+1);
    _y -= (_y-_root.Origin._y)/(random(20)+1);
    _rotation++;
    _yscale = _xscale = Math.abs(_x-_root.Origin._x)-100;
}
```

One of the greatest things about Flash MX is the ability to target clipEvents *remotely*. We could write these clipEvents on the root, but we don't. The reason why is that when we create the duplicates, we want them *all* to have these actions. If the actions are on the movie clip and then it's duplicated, they will all carry onto the duplicate. But, if we try to target, we need to write a for statement to send the actions 60 times to each movie clip. This would not work very well, so we use old style clipEvent locations.

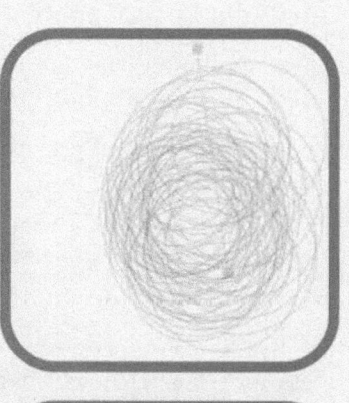

As for the actual code, we have nothing too complex here. We initialize the locations to the location of Origin (which is moving about), as in _x = _root.Origin._x. Then, on each frame passage, we set properties. We start with the x and the y again by subtracting the distance from themselves to the Origin MC. To that we then divide by a random value. This all looks like: _x -= (_x-_root.Origin._x)/(Math.random(20)+1). Next, we set the rotation to continually count incrementally. Lastly, we again use the distance, but this time we use Math.abs to make sure that the value is a positive value. Then we minus 100. This becomes the scale.

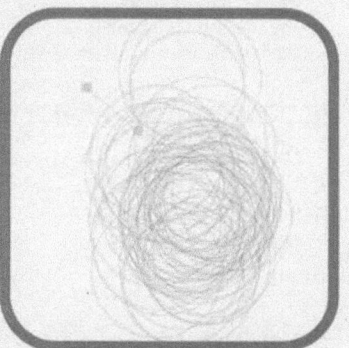

Save this as a new version named 'B_02.fla' and export (or refer to the file B_02.fla). We get a much more dynamic engine now.

As an interesting variation here, we can try adding a fill in Node3.

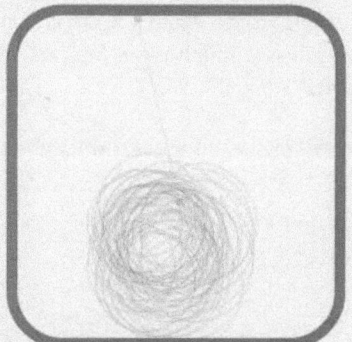

For the next iteration, we will make one small change to make the entire thing fully interactive. We can make it drag on both axes by writing this:

```
_quality = "low";
fscommand(allowscale="false");
loadMovieNum("audio/03.swf", 10);
stop();

this.onEnterFrame = function() {
    // Replicate
    if (C<59) {
        _root.Node.duplicateMovieClip("Node"+C, C);
        C++;
    }
    // Dragger
    if (MD) {
        _root.Drag._x = _root._xmouse;
    }
    // Elastic Engine
    TXn = (TXn*.96)+(_root.Drag._x-_root.Origin._x)*.05;
    TYn = (TYn*.96)+(_root.Drag._y-_root.Origin._y)*.05;
    _root.Origin._x += (TXn+(_level10.amp[_level10._currentframe]*.5));
    _root.Origin._y += (TYn+(_level10.amp[_level10._currentframe]*.5));
    // Draw Lines
    this.createEmptyMovieClip("Draw", C+100000);
    Draw.lineStyle(.25, 0xFF3399, 25);
    Draw.moveTo(_root.Origin._x, _root.Origin._y);
    Draw.lineTo(_root.Drag._x, _root.Drag._y);
};
this.onMouseDown = function() {
    MD = 1;
};
this.onMouseUp = function() {
    MD = 0;
};
```

Here we have simply created elasticity code for the y axis also. We changed a few values; like the .96 (which was .95) and the .05 (which was .025). Also, we have added the "amp" audio values to the x and y so that the audio makes the entire thing "bounce". What we get as a result is a much more interactive toy. We can now drag it around in any direction and do what we want with it.

Save this as a new version named 'B_03.fla' and export (or refer to the file B_03.fla).

The last thing we are going to look into is a playful little toy that I have begun working on. This is not done, and truthfully, I'm not even sure where I want to go with it. But, nonetheless, I thought it would be a good thing to share. I am not going to go into a lot of detail on how this actually works because the difficult parts have been covered already. My advice is to look into this file and see what makes it tick. This is actually quite an easy file to understand without guidance because most of it is hard-coded (meaning that it isn't dynamic or in built on-the-fly).

Basically, Project C is a stickman that dances. We use the audio in pretty much the same way as we have in the last two projects, only this time we make something a bit different. The only real trick here is that we need to establish the rules and relationships that govern the body structure of the figure. Once the figure knows how it is assembled, we can let it dance.

The following goes on the root:

```
_quality = "low";
fscommand(allowscale="false");
loadMovieNum("audio/05.swf", 10);
_ = .5;
_ = .5;
ange = 40;
this.onLoad = function() {
    for (N=1; N<7; N++) {
        // Replicate
        Nav.duplicateMovieClip("Nav"+N, N);
        _root["Nav"+N]._x = (N*11)+156;
        _root["Nav"+N].MyNumber = N;
    }
}
stop();

this.onEnterFrame = function() {
    LineWidth = .25;
    LineAlpha = 25;
    LineColor = 0xFF3399;
    // LeftLeg
    this.createEmptyMovieClip("LeftTibia", 101);
    LeftTibia.lineStyle(LineWidth, LineColor, LineAlpha);
    LeftTibia.moveTo(this.AnkleLeft._x, this.AnkleLeft._y);
    LeftTibia.lineTo(this.KneeLeft._x, this.KneeLeft._y);
    this.createEmptyMovieClip("LeftFemur", 102);
    LeftFemur.lineStyle(LineWidth, LineColor, LineAlpha);
    LeftFemur.moveTo(this.KneeLeft._x, this.KneeLeft._y);
    LeftFemur.lineTo((this.Hips._x-(this.Hips._width/2)), this.Hips._y);
    // RightLeg
    this.createEmptyMovieClip("RightTibia", 103);
    RightTibia.lineStyle(LineWidth, LineColor, LineAlpha);
```

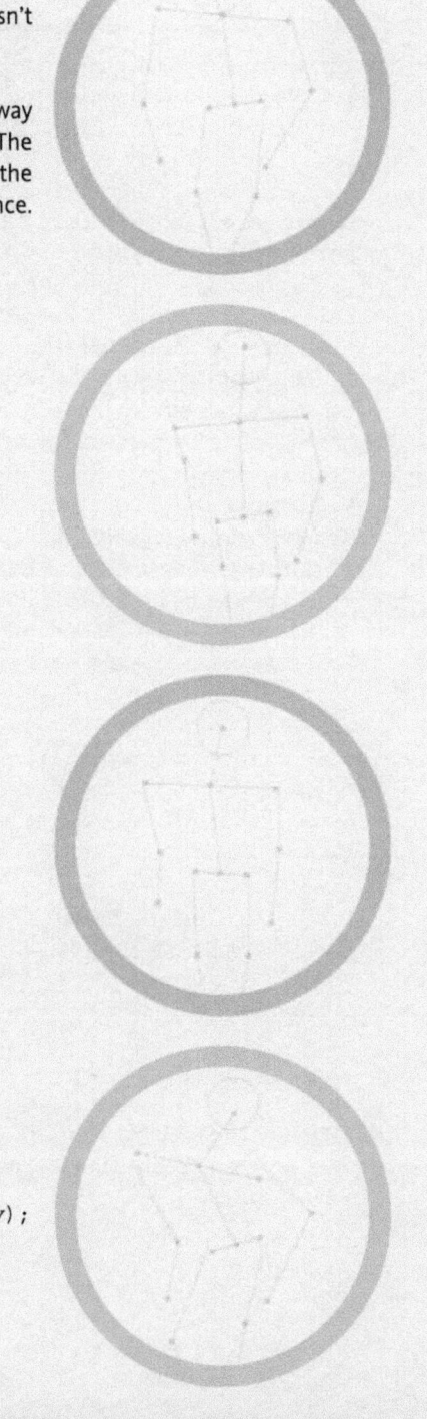

```
    RightTibia.moveTo(this.AnkleRight._x, this.AnkleRight._y);
    RightTibia.lineTo(this.KneeRight._x, this.KneeRight._y);
    this.createEmptyMovieClip("RightFemur", 104);
    RightFemur.lineStyle(LineWidth, LineColor, LineAlpha);
    RightFemur.moveTo(this.KneeRight._x, this.KneeRight._y);
    RightFemur.lineTo((this.Hips._x+(this.Hips._width/2)),  this.Hips._y);
    // LeftArm
    this.createEmptyMovieClip("LeftRadius", 105);
    LeftRadius.lineStyle(LineWidth, LineColor, LineAlpha);
    LeftRadius.moveTo(this.WristLeft._x, this.WristLeft._y);
    LeftRadius.lineTo(this.ElbowLeft._x, this.ElbowLeft._y);
    this.createEmptyMovieClip("LeftHumerous", 106);
    LeftHumerous.lineStyle(LineWidth, LineColor, LineAlpha);
    LeftHumerous.moveTo(this.ElbowLeft._x, this.ElbowLeft._y);
    LeftHumerous.lineTo((this.Shoulders._x-(this.Shoulders._width/2)), this.Shoulders._y);
    // RightArm
    this.createEmptyMovieClip("RightRadius", 107);
    RightRadius.lineStyle(LineWidth, LineColor, LineAlpha);
    RightRadius.moveTo(this.WristRight._x, this.WristRight._y);
    RightRadius.lineTo(this.ElbowRight._x, this.ElbowRight._y);
    this.createEmptyMovieClip("RightHumerous", 108);
    RightHumerous.lineStyle(LineWidth, LineColor, LineAlpha);
    RightHumerous.moveTo(this.ElbowRight._x, this.ElbowRight._y);
    RightHumerous.lineTo((this.Shoulders._x+(this.Shoulders._width/2)), this.Shoulders._y);
    // Spine
    this.createEmptyMovieClip("Spine", 109);
    Spine.lineStyle(LineWidth, LineColor, LineAlpha);
    Spine.moveTo(this.Shoulders._x, this.Shoulders._y);
    Spine.lineTo(this.Hips._x, this.Hips._y);
    // Head
    this.createEmptyMovieClip("Skull", 110);
    Skull.lineStyle(LineWidth, LineColor, LineAlpha);
    Skull.moveTo(this.Shoulders._x, this.Shoulders._y);
    Skull.lineTo(this.Head._x, this.Head._y);
};
```

And, the following goes on each joint movie clip:

```
onClipEvent (load) {
    XD = _x;
    YD = _y;
}
onClipEvent (enterFrame) {
    TXn = (TXn*_root.F)+(XD-_x)*_root.V;
    _x += TXn;
    TYn = (TYn*_root.F)+(YD-_y)*_root.V;
    _y += TYn;
    TRn = (TRn*_root.F)+(0-_rotation)*_root.V;
```

```
    _rotation += TRn;
    if (_level10.amp[_level10._currentframe]>40) {
        TXn += (random(_root.Range)-(_root.Range/2));
        TYn += (random(_root.Range)-(_root.Range/2));
        TRn += (random(_root.Range)-(_root.Range/2));
    }
}
```

A lot of this will look familiar, some will not. All in all, it is pretty simple to dissect.

If we refer to the file B_03.fla, we see the figure assemble and the figure reacting...

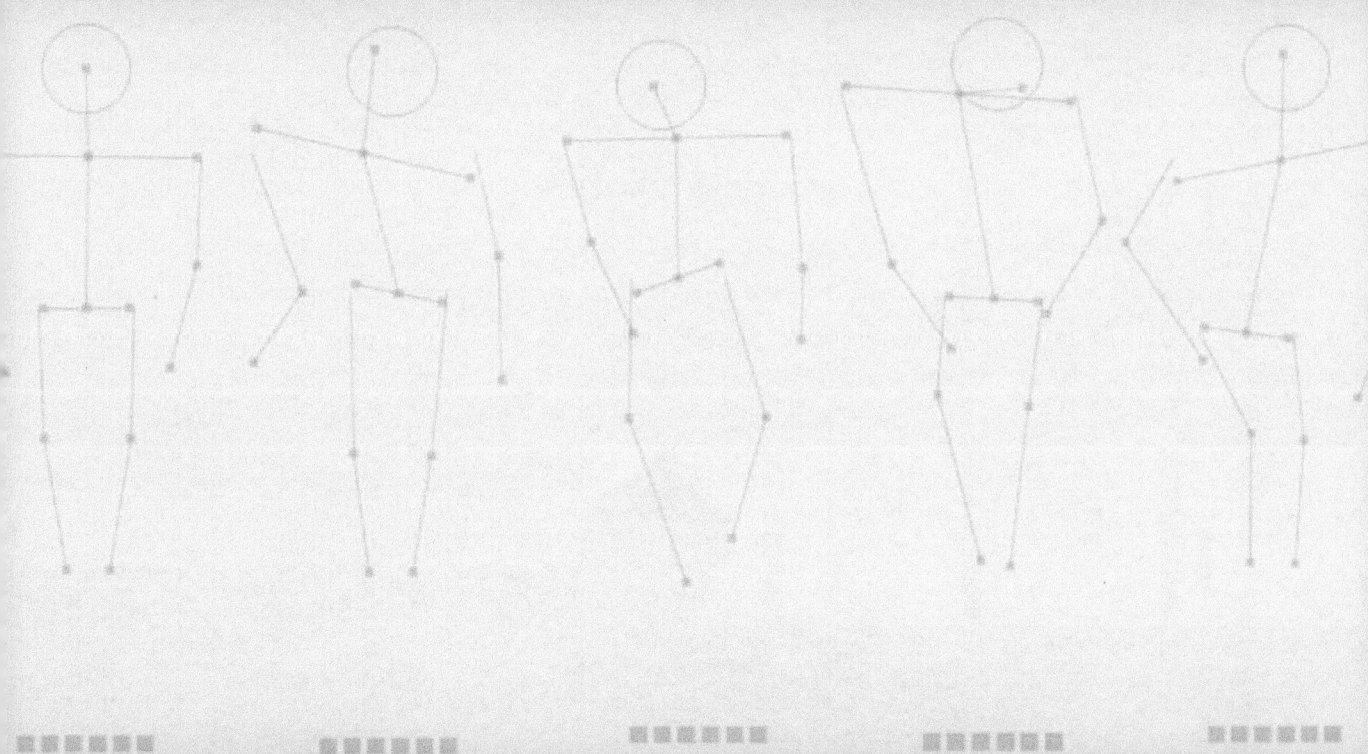

All this really consists of is a bunch of movie clips arranged as the joints (Head, Neck, Shoulders, Elbows, Wrists, Hips, Knees and Ankles) of a human body. We connect the joints with lines as we handled the lines in Project A and B. Then we make each joint react to the audio stream... and that's really all there is to this. The joints use the same elasticity code as Project B did, so really, *nothing* here is new. Even the movie clips are the same.

And that's it. Explore this file. Figure it out. Change it. Break it. Fix it. Rebuild it. Whatever. The best thing to do is to just get into it. As long as you are exploring, you are learning.

If you have any questions or need assistance with any of this code, you may e-mail me at support@soundofdesign.com with a subject line of "Sound Re-Activity".

points, lines, and movement
jd hooge

There are a lot of ways to achieve the same goal using Flash. I try to keep my code as streamlined as possible. There are many ways to refine your code and your files, such as using loops, functions, and few graphics on the stage. Also, it is very important to limit how many operations are running constantly...

This project is simply an experiment that dives into several new Flash MX techniques and methods. Our main goal in this project is to plot out the lines and points of specific shapes, I'm going to use a circle, a triangle and a star. This example uses points (movie clips attached from the Library) and lines (drawn with the drawing API methods) to draw our shapes. After we have achieved that goal, we'll start to explore a few other techniques to enhance the result.

We build an '**Array Recorder**', which allows us to click several points to make a shape. The points' coordinates are recorded into arrays. Then, we take those arrays into a new FLA, and loop through the coordinates placing a movie clip at each point. Lastly, we connect the points with lines. This is done using the moveTo and lineTo methods.

After we have created our shape, we'll experiment with a few other techniques.

The first is to add another line to each point, which curves to a central point or hub. This is done using the moveTo and curveTo methods.

The second step will be to experiment with applying different types of programmatic motion to our points.

Third, we'll add an element of interactivity by allowing the user to change from one shape to the next, creating a morphing effect.

Fourth, we'll play around with the new dynamic masking feature (the setMask method).

Lastly, we will add a final touch by applying elastic scaling motion to the points, creating a bouncing effect.

Typically, I like to run my Flash files on LOW quality. However, in this project, I am using a lot of circles that don't render well when aliased, so I have kept all of the files on HIGH quality. Feel free to switch the quality to LOW during the tutorial to see the performance difference. Let's dive in and get Flashing!

The array recorder

Our array recorder is a separate Flash file that allows us to click several points to form a shape. The points' coordinates are recorded into arrays so we can use them in our design:

Start a new movie and set the movie size to 400 x 600 and the Frame Rate to 40 fps. The first thing you want to create is the grid that you'll use as your drawing area. My grid is set to 380 x 380. The grid is made up of vertical and horizontal lines that are 20 pixels apart. Before you move on, turn your grid into a movie clip, name it Grid, place it on the stage at (10, 10) and give it the instance name Grid.

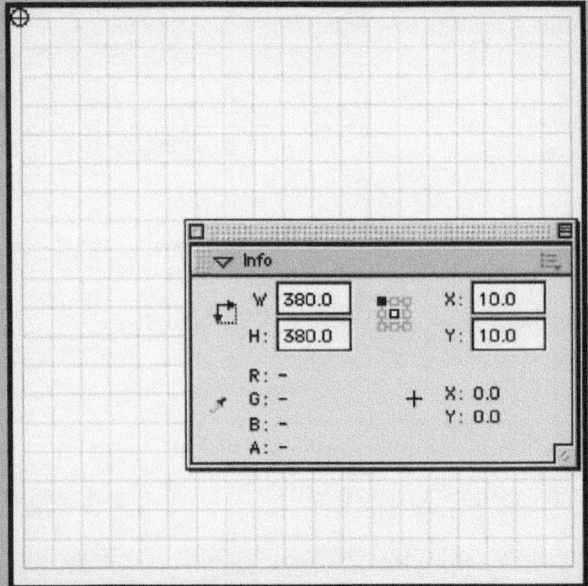

Below your grid, you'll have some space left over, which we'll use to display the coordinates. Create two dynamic text fields and give them variable names display_x and display_y respectively.

Now you are going to create your point. Create a new movie clip and name it Point. Make sure you use the advanced settings and check the box that reads Export for ActionScript. This allows you to attach that clip from the Library by referring to that name. Now go into the empty movie clip and create a small circle with the dimensions 8 x 8, making sure that the zero point is centered.

Now you have all the elements you need to begin building the engine for the recorder.